THIS WORLD, MY HOME

BY WALTER LOCKE

Whistling Post, Ohio
A Cash Transaction
Halcyon Days

This World, My Home

Walter Locke

THE ANTIOCH PRESS, YELLOW SPRINGS, 1957

67944

Copyright 1957
THE ANTIOCH PRESS

Library of Congress
Catalog Card Number
57-12038

Printed in the United States of America
by The Antioch Press, Yellow Springs, Ohio

To the old who have shared with me this changeful, triumphant, tragical world, our home—yet more to the young who must cope with the challenging, perilous, hopeful world to come—I devote these glimpses of tomorrow's yesterday.

Walter Locke is as sensitive to America's meaning—all of America's meanings—as any living man. And no one has told us what we are, who we are, and why we are as we are, with more grace and grandeur. I am grateful that this wise and gentle man has been persuaded to write this important book.

—Adlai E. Stevenson

Walter Locke: For thirty years we have journeyed together in the joys of our profession. His solid philosophy, tempered by kindness and qualities of real affection, has given me a treasured companion; his breadth of knowledge, reaching deep into history, politics and literature, created one of the conspicuous writers of his time. He is known for his purity of diction, his rugged intellectual integrity and courage, and a conciousness of duty which falls on one blessed with talents.

—James M. Cox

Contents

Introduction

ALTHOUGH WALTER LOCKE is only eighty-two years old by the calendar, his life has bridged three centuries of American civilization. I had better document that astonishing statement. He was born in 1875 in a log cabin in the West Virginia hills where his mother, father and neighbors lived much in the style of the Plymouth and Jamestown settlers.

In other parts of America the post-Civil War industrial expansion was radically altering the pattern of life. Industrial organizations were accumulating the power that individuals had held in their own right when America was new. But the citizens of Pleasant County, West Virginia, were hardly aware of the violent changes that were taking place in the North and the West. They raised their food in kitchen gardens, sawed logs to make barrel staves for the market, maintained their families as units with spinning, weaving and the other household crafts and read the Bible and *Pilgrim's Progress,* and the children went barefoot except in winter. Elder Brewster would have been comfortable in that environment.

When Mr. Locke was still a boy, his father moved the family to Nebraska where the reckless nineteenth century was creating another civilization of railroad politics and crop farming for the cash market. As a boy and youth on the prairie Mr. Locke learned other parts of the American saga—breaking rock by hand in a stone quarry, selling newspapers, farming, teaching district school and eventually joining the staff of the *Nebraska State Journal* in Lincoln.

Mr. Locke was fifty-one when he plunged head-first into the twentieth century. At the invitation of Governor James M. Cox, he became editor of the Dayton *Daily News* in the heart of a restless industrial complex. "Life for me was just beginning," he says of his arrival in Dayton in 1927. For the next twenty-seven years he was immersed in the ideas, problems, enterprise and power of modern America. Three years ago he relinquished his post as editor, continuing only with his column, "Trends of the Times," maintained without a break for thirty years, which appears five days a week in the Cox newspapers in Ohio, Georgia and Florida.

During the winter months Mr. and Mrs. Locke live in Miami. During the rest of the year they live in a four-room log cabin in a fifteen-acre patch of woods and wild growth that is only six miles from the center of Dayton. This cabin, and a second cabin built later, were originally intended as a weekend retreat. But in 1942 Mr. and Mrs. Locke tired of the city, modernized the cabins and established their permanent quarters there. Their living is scarcely of the seventeenth century, but it retains much of the simplicity that has been lost elsewhere in our land.

This unique range of experience would be only a curiosity if Mr. Locke were not a unique man. He is. He knows the significance of what he has been through. Although he has climbed out of old civilizations into the newest one, he has not forgotten what he has learned. He has not forgotten the people, the customs or the moral states of mind. All these civilizations live in him simultaneously. For he is a reflective writer. As a newspaper editor, he has been concerned with politics and has been occasionally involved in interesting political situations. But never at the expense of the things he loves—nature (birds particularly), poetry, literature, music, religion and history.

Although he is a modest man who feels uncomfortable about the first person singular pronoun, he is an American sage who has more knowledge than most people and a deeper perspective than any man I know. He loves America. In general, he approves of the twentieth century resurgence. But he is aware of and concerned with the unevenness of a technological development that has outgrown its spiritual strength. He avoids theological terms. But he is a person of such moral grandeur that there are strong religious overtones in his concluding chapter about the weaknesses of America today.

During his early career as a school-teacher, Mr. Locke once served as "disciplinarian" in a school for the Seminoles in what was then known as Indian Territory. Like everything else that came his way, it added to his store of wisdom. "Among these aboriginal Americans, I was to live in the time of Homer or, who knows, in the time of Moses or Methuselah," he observes. That unconscious marriage of poet and prophets in one sentence is both happy and illuminating. For this is a book by a poet and a prophet.

Technically, it is autobiography. But it is also a social and spiritual history of America. It is written by the only man who has the experience, the purity of character and the literary skill to render such an account of our national life. The account balances.

BROOKS ATKINSON

New York City

THIS WORLD, MY HOME

1

My Aunt Lide, her home

MY AUNT LIDE was out by the woodpile chopping sticks for the supper fire. As she swung the ax, in the woman's awkward way with an implement made for a man, she was singing in her high, thin, sweet voice:

> *This world's a wilderness of woe,*
> *This world is not my home.*

There was more to it, something about laying her armor down and resting in peace at home. By "home" my Aunt Lide was not thinking of her cabin with its wood to be cut and the twin babies to be fed. That was her earthly habitation, not the place of heavenly rest she was sighing and singing for.

Life, though simple, was hard in the West Virginia hills when my Aunt Lide was middle-aged and I a wondering child. The woodpile was only one of the endless trials of the Aunt Lides of that land. The men, with their own work to do, scrambling around the hills, were forever forgetting their domestic duty with the ax. Supper time would come and no wood for the kitchen stove. What Aunt Lide anywhere would not then be wishing this wilderness of woe wiped out and the world of her yearning won?

For this world, as my Aunt Lide was wrestling with it seventy-five years ago, there was no slightest hope. Life in it was a losing game. Her world, that day of the vanishing hoopskirt, was a forest whose white oaks and pines were yielding to lesser breeds of trees. The axes of the men, however laggard with the kitchen wood, echoed lustily in the forest the year around. They felled the taller trees, leaving the hill slopes to the scrub. With monstrous labor of grub hoe and ax the men had made clearings where a bit of garden and a patch of grain could grow. Here was a wondrous soil, the saved-up leaf mould of scores of centuries. That soil nature had tenderly nursed and reared. The roots of the trees had encircled and held it safe from spoiling by its raging enemies, the rain and wind and melting snow. Now it was left exposed, like an unwanted child left on a wild mountainside to die.

The winds blew and the floods came and beat upon that soil. Quickly, swiftly, it flowed into French Creek, on to the Ohio, on to the Mississippi, at last to choke the Gulf of Mexico. We know, without clear labor of mind, when our world is moving up or slipping down. Our spirits reflect it though we know it not. My Aunt Lide, hacking at the woodpile with her ax, was sad, as she had a right to be, in that decadent economy. Her world was a wilderness of woe. This world was not her home. Singing so despondently of this world, her hope deferred to a world beyond the graveyard crowning the near-by hill, my Aunt Lide did not know, of course, of the coming flood of oil.

Men long had dreamed, in those hills, not only of the heaven above to which my Aunt Lide looked, but of a nearer paradise, and one more practical. One might at long last strike sweet music from a heavenly harp; but why wait? They might here and now strike oil. They sang with old Omar, of whom they had not heard: "Ah, take the cash and let the credit go."

They had their will. Before my Aunt Lide was much older, oil was gushing from her hills. What mattered, then, the wasted soil, the squandered oaks and pines? With the oil came gas. Gas emerged in such surplus they left it flaming from the pipes the day and year around. The emancipation of my Aunt Lide! The ax lay rusting in the shed. The supper fire, like the sacred flame the vestal virgins tended in the temple of old Rome, was never out. Here was a kitchen paradise.

The child who had listened as his Aunt Lide, hacking the supper wood, despaired of this world, had gone on west ere the flow of oil began. The years, as we see them foreshortened by the backward look, slipped fast away. The boy had found in the virgin prairie a hope denied him in the hills. There we were breaking sod for access to the rich leavings of aeons of living, dying grass. There men were still fattening on the free buffalo.

This new world wilderness had, of course, its own woes. The grasshoppers came in clouds. There was that dread day in July when a flaming south wind crisped the growing corn. But this new world was growing. We lived for the look ahead. If it was a wilderness, it was, unlike my Aunt Lide's world, in her kindling-chopping days, a wilderness of hope.

The speeding years slipped past—a score, two score of them. My Aunt Lide who sang so sweetly, sadly at the woodpile when the greying man was but a thoughtless boy, what would she be saying, singing, now? I must go back to see. A thousand miles behind me, I puff my way to the hilltop where my Aunt Lide, long past all chopping wood, all supper getting, sits waiting. She is waiting, but not for me or any man. And what is this, in a thin, cracked, sweet voice she is singing still? As at her chopping, years and years ago: "This world's a wilderness of woe; this world is not my home." The oil, following the oaks, is gone. Even while it lasted it could not make a home for my Aunt Lide. This world, no matter what it held, was not her home. Now, this world's sands run out, she was sitting, smiling, singing, awaiting her call, not long ahead, to the home she was yearning for.

2

The world of my father and mother

MY FATHER WAS A GOOD HAND WITH THE AX. He needed to be.
By way of the ax and crosscut saw our simple living lay. Oak
staves for the cooper, pine logs for the sawmill, cross-ties for the
railroads and bark for the tannery—these, with a little hillside
farming, were our whole stock in trade.

To wield the ax and hold the end of a crosscut saw was a
man's job, nothing less. But in the woods where the men worked
was work, too, for a boy. There was the bark to peel from the
logs cut by the saw. The staves, as they were split, were to be
put in piles. The lengths of tanbark stripped from trees felled
for their bark alone must be laid in ricks. When land was being
cleared, the brush grubbed up must be thrown, for the burning,
into heaps. All this a boy could do.

Then there was that recurring desolation for a boy, the ax to
grind. The woodsman carried a whetstone in his coat. From time
to time as the day went on he would pause in his chopping to
whet his ax. This answered for the day. In the end, the whetstone was not enough. A major operation was required. There
lay the boy's job—the grindstone was his to turn.

My father was christened Francis Marion for the hit-and-
away hero of the Revolution. He was the mildest man ever named
for the wildest man. I knew him well for almost sixty years. In
all that time I never knew him to quarrel or fight or argue with
any man. He was the soul of patience. The grindstone was to
teach me that. Together we worked, I at the crank, he with ax
in hand. What followed was doubtless no more than an hour or
so. To me it was an eternity. Round and round the grindstone
went, a war of stone on steel. My father, after an age or two,
would remove the ax from the stone, giving my weary arm a
rest. He would test its edge with his thumb while I watched in
hopeful fear. He would shake his head—he was a man of few

words or none—then the dreary round again. My hope deferred, I might groan and whine. My father would not be moved. Here was a labor to be done aright. He would stop when the ax was razor-edged and not a whit before.

Few small boys of my time and place missed this educational experience. Their lamentations have passed into the language. An age that hardly knows what a grindstone is (or was) employs the word today as a symbol of dull, slow toil. It was indeed a dull and "grinding" toil, turning the grindstone for my father's ax. Nothing I have ever been called to do has seemed more desolately monotonous. And through the years that were to follow I have still been grinding, as all men must. And if I have worked a little overtime, trying to make better what would pass as good enough, I ascribe it to those eternities at the grindstone where my father kept his faith with his ax and with himself.

Out in the woods, day after day, week after week, we worked together, my father and I. With his frow he split the staves. I piled them up. With the ax we had sharpened I stripped the "cuts" of their bark. I hurried to get ahead of him. Then, while he was catching up, I could hunt for May apples and ginseng roots, or set a rabbit trap.

There was little talking. There was small need to talk. We understood each other, my father and I, with little use of words. He never argued. I could not "talk back" to him, of course, even had I wanted to. Children in those days did not "sass" their parents, not if they cared to keep their heads on straight. There in the woods my father and I worked together and came to know each other well. There we formed a friendship that held fast until he died. Never in all our life together did a harshness mar our companionship. If there were impatient thoughts they passed off unexpressed.

What thoughts filled my father's mind through the sixty years of our friendship there is no way to tell. He was born into his party and stayed there to the end. He joined his church before I was born and stayed there, too, till its time came to bury him. But he gave his thought no tongue. I knew him by his actions, not by his words. He had his work in the woods and kept at it till the woods were gone. He went west to a job as a stone quarryman and stayed with that till the stone was gone. He became a farmer and farmed till his life was gone.

I babble more words in a year than he in his lifetime, yet my education at his hands went on unceasingly. He was as potent a teacher as ever small boy had. If I were to word my worry about the small boys of today, it would be this: What chance have they to grow up with their fathers, go to school to their fathers, become friends of their fathers, be steadied by their fathers' hands and heads and hearts?

His nurse came to my aged father's bedside as he lay suffering, weak. A famous trial, a kidnaping, had gone to the jury. The Hauptman jury, the nurse said, has come in. My father wanly smiled. "I wish," he said, "my jury would come in."

Deep in that night his jury came in. My father had taken his death, like his life, in his quiet, steady stride.

My mother was washing the dishes. A boy still in dresses (boys in the 1870's wore dresses till three or four years old) was watching her. There my memory of my mother begins.

Scarce was I out of dresses when I was washing the dishes and my mother was watching me. Unlike my father, my mother would bring written authority to bear. As I washed the dishes she was quoting this to me:

> *Train up a child in the way he should go;*
> *and when he is old he will not depart from it.*

Ancient wisdom had discerned that truth, and here one small boy was, washing dishes accordingly.

I was washing dishes, trained in the way I should go, from that time forth. For pure odiousness, washing wishes and turning the grindstone were all one to any boy. To magnify the discipline, if it wasn't dishes to wash, it was beans in the garden to hoe. If it wasn't beans to hoe in the garden, it was chips to pick up in the woodyard behind the house.

Chips! Chips for the kitchen fire, with my mother, were a passion never appeased. Chips from the wood-chopping dried quickly and burned hot and fast. Chips were forever called for to hasten the dinner fire. I was the chip bearer to the queen. It was wearying to the back, this picking up of chips. But along with the dish-washing and bean-hoeing it got me acquainted with my mother. Even as I grew to friendship with my father in the work of the woods, so in the yard, picking up chips, I came to know my mother.

My mother's grandfather Shields was born in Tipperary. Her mother Shriver was Pennsylvania Dutch. Out of that admixture of opposites came a lady who was everything my Swedish-Scotch-English father was not. She had the tongue my father lacked. We were never left ignorant of what my mother thought. My father, once he got going at anything, never stopped. He circled in his orbit as steady as the moon around the earth. But he needed a starter. My self-starting mother supplied, sometimes with a certain prodding, my father's deficiency.

I had hardly got farther in letters than Mary's little lamb when my mother led me to the source of her authority concerning my bringing up. That was the only book, indeed, save my McGuffey *Reader* and Rev. Randall's book of travel in the Holy Land, the family possessed. It would be a proper use of my new knowledge of the alphabet, she urged, if I would read that big book through. From cover to cover I should read it through. After all the dish washing and all the work in the woods, there was plenty of time left. Through the books of Genesis, Exodus, Leviticus, Numbers, Deuteronomy and on and on I sped. What could it all mean to a boy of seven years? Little more, no doubt, than a vague idea that I'd better be good. I could lose my Eden or be drowned in a flood. A people could keep the straight and narrow path and thrive, or go off the track and die. Wasn't that something to learn and profit by?

If my "neck 'n ears" are ever clean today, it is because my mother fixed my habits then. Her instructions with the broom after the dishes had been washed led to the post, a little later, of schoolhouse janitor, my business beginning. Her proddings sent me forth to shovel the neighbor's snow for quarters bigger than any dollar measures now. She spanked me lovingly as my sins required, but she fed me and clothed me and sat up late on a Saturday night to knit the warm new mittens for next day's Sunday school. She mourned sorrowingly when I mourned and rejoiced when I rejoiced.

When the work in the woods failed in the West Virginia hills, it was my mother urged my father off to a post on the western plains. When the quarry work failed, she fed her family by feeding boarders till other work was found. When, at the early age of seventy, she left her tired body, there fell upon me a desolation such as any man can know but once.

There had been in my world one being who had always thought of me before herself. One friend who would never forsake me, however good or bad I might be, had been granted me. Wherever I was, whatever I did, she would be with me, helping me.

Now that one was gone. There could never be another such. Devoted friends and loving family there could be, but a mother, only one!

"I stand upon the summit of my years" and take the long backward look. From ax and saw and ox cart to the electronic age stretch the years of one life. The year just past, as I look, I can hardly distinguish from the year before or the years leading up to that. The nearer decades lie, as I look backward, an even monotone. Something special stirred me when I turned fifty. Life, I then discovered, must some day have a stop. Life set a landmark when I took a wife and when the small son came.

Yet on the whole, my life at the backward look runs like a gently rolling prairie land, till, presto! What is this?

Sky-high as the distance gathers, a shining mountain range of years appears. Clearer and fairer than this very morning's light they loom, those years, no more than a handful, when I lived with my father in the woods, with my mother washing dishes in the house. Here was the bringing up from which, whether or not in the way he should go, the child does not depart when he is old.

3

This world beyond

FROM MY GRANDMOTHER'S HOUSE on Nine Mile Ridge, where my memory begins, I could throw a stone at the setting sun and land it in French Creek far below. If I cast my stone at the rising sun it would roll into Painter Creek. In other directions lay Long's Run and Shawnee and McKim. Endlessly beyond them rose fold after fold of hills with their own creeks and "runs" between, for hillsides must shed their rain. For aught a boy could see, my world was an infinity of hollows and of hills. Through the haze overhanging it I could see that it was there, this world of hollows and of hills. But that was all. What fields, what peoples, what towns were hidden there?

Beneath the ceiling of blue a curtain of green was hung, the forest, impenetrable to the eye. Beyond the walls of intervening hills, beneath that screen of trees lay a world unknown to me. What was that world like? What was to do but set forth and see?

The dull and listless grown-up man, his birthright trail of glory long ago grown dim, might answer. Look about you. See these stones and trees and hill slopes near at hand. The misty distance which you cannot see is only more of them. These plodding men and harried women and hallooing children familiar to you here will be around you just the same if you journey over there. Cease your wondering, wandering. Stay at home. Here you see all there is to see.

What blindness, but for the second sight of children, would be binding us here on earth! These old folk, saying wisdom dies with them! Saying what, with their failing eyes, they see around them, is all there is to see! The small boy on the ridge, straining his eyes for endless other heights beyond the sunrise and beside the sunset, could not be deceived by such adult shortsightedness. Let them be blind. He would see.

What magic cities, what lovely lakes, what mighty men and lovely women those dim hills and hidden valleys might contain! "There were giants in those days," I had read in the ancient Book my mother had given me. Why not giants on those far off hills and in the valleys which the hills have hid?

On autumn nights I could see on the horizon fires started in the forest from the brush heaps burned in the clearings by all too careless men. What matter! The woods rolled on in a boundless sea. What could a fire subtract from infinity?

To the boy, the fire on the far hilltop but added enchantment to the mystery he was bound to penetrate. I wanted to set out to find that fire. What manner of men surrounded those flames? What cities were in its path? What peoples, what works of men lay over there?

From the north and west on frosty mornings there floated across the hills deep-throated calls as if some mighty monster were raging through the land. It was, indeed, as I was to learn, a monster. It was a steamboat breasting the current of the Ohio on its way to Wheeling or Pittsburgh with freight and passengers. The men of the Ridge knew each steamboat by its whistled voice. I, having never seen a river or a boat, was free to build in my dream rivers and boats of such majesty as never was.

From the south and east, on those same mornings, came shrieking cries as of a mightier monster in distress. The small boy was soon to leave his hills, riding the railroad train with the shrilling voice. Till then, the rushing monster was circumscribed in speed and sound only by the boyish awe the sound aroused.

From our ridge I could see far; but what I could see was little to the hidden part. The houses were out of sight in the hollows or buried beneath the trees. Such as I could see were apt to be beyond the range of my traveling. Who lived in those houses, what they were like, was for a wondering boy to dream out for himself. When the people came to church, a revival or a burial, it was as if the earth had opened to give up its living, not its dead. By shaded footpath or sled-worn trail they came from nowhere; from the vast emptiness of hollows, hills and woods.

There were caves in those hills, as I knew from my own wandering. What lurked deep in their darkness? I hurried past them

fearfully. I had heard terrifying bed-time tales of panthers heard
by men who found themselves belated on a mountain after dark.

The more I could not see, the more enchanting the mystery.
The old men cackled: "Stay at home; quit your wondering."
I have lived to be glad I was born to hills and hollows and woods
where the seen was as nothing to the unseen, inviting an ever-
lasting questioning. For such was to be the whole of life and
the world for me—a vast unknown, unseen, calling me away
from the seen and known.

But until his time to wander came, a boy's world in the hills
was real things as well as wonderings. My Uncle Tom owned
a hillside farm worth five dollars an acre or so. He had as many
as forty sheep, half a dozen cattle, a team of horses, a wagon.
His house was of three rooms, not one or two, as with most of us.
It was heated by a stone fireplace with mud-coated chimney of
sticks. The family boasted two feather beds. In the fall, Uncle
Tom made up, from his own cane crop, a barrel of sorghum
molasses for the family's winter sweet. He grew his own pork.
Aunt Charlotte spun and wove the wool from the family sheep.
All this made my Uncle Tom one of the wealthier men of my
world. The presence of three strong sons to help in field and
woods had its part in his prosperity.

Between the better off, like Uncle Tom, and the less well off,
like most of us, lay subtle social shades. Those who slept on
feathers were on one side, and those who, like ourselves, slept
on straw were on the other side of the "tracks." The ox-team
drivers ranked a bit below the horse-team men. I had a turnip
to top off my corn bread lunch at school. My betters had wheat
bread with apples for dessert. My social education was early
advanced when I tried to trade my turnip for the apple of another
boy. Thus early I came to know "the whips and scorns of time,
the proud man's contumely."

I once heard my Aunt Becky shaming my mother because,
as Aunt Becky said, "You haven't a feather bed to your name."
How miserably true it was! We were all poor, but some were
poorer than others of us, till it came to the Ronley family. With
the Ronleys the rating reached bottom and stopped. We all went
barefoot in spring, summer and fall. The Ronley children went

barefoot even in wintertime. That, in our hills, was the lowest in poverty.

But whatever we had not there, no one of us knew the poverty of hunger. There were always squirrels and rabbits to be caught and the turnip pits of all of us were open to any neighbor in his need. All the rest of us managed to have, in winter, one pair of boots. One pair was all. The one pair had to see us through. The coming of March found many a toe exposed. Toes open, soles worn thin, they had to do. I knew what it was to go for the cows barefoot through morning frost, delighted to find, for the comfort of numb feet, the warm spots where the animals had slept.

Such a relativity, riches! I was never again to be as wealthy as when, a youth in a Nebraska village, I was earning fifty dollars a month as a teacher while the Burlington section boss, the next most opulent citizen, was paid but forty-five dollars.

In the way of men everywhere, we had subtle gradations in our hill country poverty, yet they had no sting. In this land and time of equal opportunity men prospered according to their skill and energy. Land was cheap. The woods awaited the ax and saw of all who cared to come. Even the lame Midkiff was able, with his pedlar's pack, to make a go of things. There was no leisure class. The low, if they hustled, could rise. The high, if they did not work, would fall. We were the captains of our own fates. We were poor, but were not "sunk" in poverty.

We had, for all our scanty means, a certain security. What we had to have was within our own control. Our housing and food and largely our clothing were the work of our own hands. On labors too great for one, as in threshing grain or when a house of logs was to be "raised," the neighbors would combine. The help of our neighbors was our "social security." In the main, we could go it alone. We trapped our own rabbits, garnered our own wild grapes and walnuts and butternuts, chopped our own fuel, grew our own corn bread and the sorghum to sweeten it. It was a scanty life; but it was free.

This had its bearing on a boy. I acquired, at seven years, an ambition to escape a boy's waist with its buttons and wear suspenders as my father did. Suspenders were bought at stores. That took money, our rarest commodity. I ranged the deep, damp hollows for a summer month or two and emerged with ginseng roots enough to pay for the best suspenders thirty-five cents could buy.

The Fourth of July drew near. Had I but the wealth to celebrate! I worked a twelve-hour day for Silas McHenry, piling up the staves he "bucked." At the store I traded for five nickels the quarter I had earned. To the picnic, jingling my nickels, all happiness, I went. All day I looked for something there to buy, something as priceless as those hard-won nickels. No such thing was there. Home at night I went, the nickels jingling in my pocket still. Such a lesson in values one twelve-hour working day had taught! We who suffered such boyhood tests are given to saying we are glad for them. They brought us self reliance. They taught the worth of simple things and gave us a heart for struggling poverty wherever it appeared.

4

Cousins, salvation, sorrow

MY MOTHER, one April morning, told my sister Elsie and me to go down French Creek and tell Mrs. Bills she was wanted. We were to stay till Mrs. Bills came back. The day went pleasantly for us. For dinner we had salt-rising bread and sorghum molasses, a welcome treat. In the middle of the afternoon Mrs. Bills returned. We were to go right home, she said. A pleasant surprise was waiting for us there.

A new sister was the surprise. It was as simple and inexpensive as that for a child to be born in our hills. Nor was the subsequent cost serious. As soon as a child was six it could take a hand at hoeing the corn and picking the beans. For clothes the younger children wore what the older ones outgrew. An addition to the family was no such economic catastrophe then as it can be today.

In keeping with this free and easy birthrate, I had a dozen uncles and as many aunts and a regiment of cousins. These uncles, aunts and cousins were to be an ever-present help in every time of trouble, a cushion between me and a rugged world. So that when I showed up, a bashful boy of five, for my first day in school, it was not as a shrinking stranger in a hostile land. The land of letters was new and strange, of course, but the cousins were all old friends. There were cousins to the right of me, cousins to the left of me, cousins in front of me, instant to see that no one not of my blood should get the best of me.

Not that the cousins coddled me. There's a force and frankness permitted to cousins which no alien can well and properly employ. When Cousin Alice saw me wiping my nose on the sleeve of my coat, she was free to reproach me as no mere noncousin, restrained by rules of formal etiquette, would have dared to do. When my Aunt Ellen found me at her dinner table with hands which showed no semblance of skin, she could lead me to the wash bowl with unsuppressed severity. Had the aunt of anyone else done that to me, one more feud might have been hatched in those hills. Here I was to see how we can be tougher and more helpful with the errors of those we love, and who know we love them, than any unfriendly critic possibly can be. Of course, it need not be aunts, uncles and cousins only that we are loved by, that we love.

In that day and place we had not heard of that modern problem, the children's insecurity. So much of our juvenile delinquency (another word and worry unheard of in the hills) comes of a childhood feeling of insecurity. The little one is allowed to think that no one loves him. He sees his family, his very foundation, dissolving before his eyes. His world is crumbling about him. In his panic he suffers wounds of the spirit which distort and defeat the life he is to live.

No such "insecurity" can be where a dozen aunts and uncles and some scores of cousins are around to hold you up. They bind up the bleeding toe you stubbed. They pick you up when you fall. They set you right firmly when you go wrong! They make your world a safe and kindly place.

The heart of the boy with the many aunts and uncles is to be pierced, year after year, with the pain of their departure, one by one, from life. With each, as the years go by, he has the inevitable journeys to the churchyard to make. For each as he goes there lingers a grateful memory. As one by one they venture "over there," these balance more and more those still alive. In the end, a merciful dispensation of providence, we care less and less whether we stay here with the quick or pass on to reunion with the dead.

The aunts and uncles gradually go. The cousins, being of our own day and age, stay on. But how they scatter! The oaks and pines by which we lived in the 1870's were vanishing. The cousins must fare forth for less exhausted soils. We scattered, mostly to the West. Years would pass. A cousin would be all but forgot. Then something jogged a cousinly memory. A letter would come. Lives long parted met again. Cousins we knew as ten-year-olds report as octogenarians. What stories to fill in the decades between! A book of many pictures and many pages, if there were time to write it, for each one!

Growing up cushioned by uncles, aunts and cousins, I had, when I went forth into an alien world, my backsets, my rebuffs, to bear. The world of men as I have found it, here, there and everywhere, is not harsh, is not heartless. But the world of strangers puts on an armor it takes time to penetrate. Men wanted to see something of the inside of me before they opened their gates. When I approached them with extended hand as if they were cousins, uncles, aunts, they put up their palms as if to say, Not so fast; wait a minute; let us have a look at you.

It was disappointing; yet I had to grant that, men being as they are, it was not unwise. But I have continued to this day to wish that, even though we cannot seem to rise to that brotherhood of man we write into our creeds, we might rise, at least, to a universal cousinship.

To such a goal as this, my aunt Charlotte had her special path. On the fourth night of the winter revival at the Nine Mile church, Aunt Charlotte would show signs of restlessness. For the year past she had been bound to earth. What with her cooking, spinning, weaving, sewing and care of children, her days had been heavy, long. Now, under the spell of concentrated, continuous pulpit eloquence, my Aunt Charlotte would let go the weary load of earth and take off, unburdened, shouting her joy, for higher spheres.

The spirit that broke forth shouting in revival time was not uncommon in the hills. The sinners at the mourners' bench were expected to climax their conversion by a demonstration of uninhibited happiness. My Aunt Charlotte was one of those who, keeping the faith the routine year around, mounted readily to the skies when the revival spirit released her from earthly care.

Those stony hills were not such an easy heaven as my Aunt Charlotte or Aunt Lide, or anyone, would care to keep as her final, only home. Rich Dives had his reward on earth. Poor Lazarus mounted elsewhere. I was not once but a thousand times hearing that this world, as my Aunt Lide sang of it, was not my home. This wilderness of woe was but a camp from which to take off for a better, more permanent abode.

Which permanent abode? There was a choice of two, as the expounder of the Book was menacingly reminding us. There was the strait and narrow way which led to life; and, the terror of it, "few there be that find it." There was the wide gate and the broad way that led to destruction; and "many there be which go in thereat." Such were the alternatives, the choice each child of earth must make. Here we were, at hard labor in the hills. We would hardly care to stay in this wilderness of woe, even if we could; but it could be worse.

With pitiless power the preacher held us to the point. How little our life here mattered, save as a chance to choose between the two impending destinies! We must choose this day whom we would serve. "For what is a man profited, if he shall gain the whole world, and lose his own soul?" I, who went to church to share the excitement of the revival time and thrill with the shouting of the saved, would came away in terror. The torments of hell burned hot for me. Whither should I flee?

I was climbing the long hill from my home in the hollow of Painter Creek to the home of my Uncle Will above. A pig of the athletic build common to pigs in the acorn-eating hills darted out of the woods, into the path ahead of me. He trotted pleasantly up the path for a dozen yards or so, then vanished in the woods again. It was a revival season. I was meditating on my eternal destiny, the predicament this life imposed. The happy pig! I said. Here he enters his path of life, and there he leaves it; and that is all for him. He has, the happy pig, no soul to lose.

But neither had the pig any soul to save.

The people of my hills were human. They had their quarrels, their rivalries, their feuds. They had their gossip mongers, bullies, cheats and sneaks. Not all was loveliness, as the year wore on among the neighbors there. One bloody fight I remember, the father of a daughter calling to account a younger man. It was an issue no small boy would understand. At the top of the year's distresses, the winter of our discontent, the great revival came, the climax of the year. Everybody came.

The preacher was not slow to press his alternatives. We could die and be doomed or we could die and be glorified. On the fourth night my Aunt Charlotte, who was never in doubt of the reward awaiting her, would be shouting her joy at the opening heavens. Others soon would add their shouts to hers. By the end

of the winter the great work had been wrought. All but a handful of the most hardened had renounced the world and set foot
on the strait and narrow way.

The effect was magical. It was as if a sudden sunny shower
had cleansed a dusty earth. When one here "got" religion, his
ego, his "old Adam," fell away from him. He loved his neighbor
even as himself. He lived, not to be served, but to serve. By that
simple somersault of the spirit our sorrows were turned to joy.
Old quarrels were reconciled, old hates annulled. Love abounded
everywhere. What mattered it then the hills were steep, the
labor hard!

This altitude was too high for many to maintain. While it
lasted it was glorious. If in time we lapsed back to the old self-
serving way, there remained the sample miracle to witness what
could be.

Life among us has grown longer and easier since those old
days in the hills. In our greater comfort we think now less of
heaven, more of earth. Some smile at those old-time noisy leaps
for paradise, a skeptical, condescending smile. But the question
of the man and his destiny and his way with other men still
presses now, as then.

Man's destiny, and woman's, was a real and ever-present issue
in those hills. When my Aunt Charlotte died on a March midnight in the year 1884, a score of neighbor men were standing
in sympathetic silence in the yard before her door. Half as many
women were intent, inside, on easing the ebbing life.

The women inside were fewer than the men without because
they had taken turns. Night and day their labor of love had run.
Those who had spent the night before in attendance were now
at home, asleep, regaining strength for wakeful nights to come.
Throughout the illness of my Aunt Charlotte the women, her
neighbors, had assumed her every household task. They had
served the meals for the stricken family. They had kept the house,
with their sweeping and dusting, immaculate.

The men, meanwhile, had lifted from the shoulders of my
grieving Uncle Tom all burden of outside work. They had
chopped the wood for the household fire. When there was
nothing left in the woodyard, they went to the woods for more.

When the midnight call came, all sound, all motion for a moment ceased. In the presence of death all men are dumb. Then all was action again. The women prepared the body for burial. The younger men set off in the dark with mattocks and spades for the all-night labor of adding one more to the church-yard's multiplying graves. Long before dawn a sound of saw and hammer rose from the shop of McClellan, the carpenter. A casket of boards, to be draped in black by the women, would be ready for the burial.

This self-forgetful kindness would have been the same for the aunt of anyone. No soul, going forth on its final adventure, in that region of neighborly good will in the West Virginia hills, was left to go forth alone. March, with its new grave, passed into April and my Grandfather Shields was sick. "The" war had ended only nineteen years before. My Irish grandfather had rashly hurrahed for the losing side in the presence of the winning side and was packed off promptly to an army jail. When he emerged at last he was a broken-bodied man, never to be strong again. Another spring had come and who was there to clear my grandfather's little field and plant his crop of corn? Who was there? Every one was there. All the neighbors came. The men brought mattocks, cant hooks, plows; the women came with hams and chickens, and potatoes from the pit where they had been buried to defy the winter frost. Prodigiously the men labored in the field against rock and clod and log. They performed as prodigiously at the ring of the dinner bell. Before the April day was done the field was cleared, plowed, planted. The hills and hollows resounded with hearty shouting of friendly farewells as the work of tired and happy people ended and the descending sun dismissed a perfect day.

We had our neighborly "raisings," too, to bring us into such oneness as only a war emergency seems able, and then but briefly, to do for us today. Youth, in that poor country, could not wait on fortune for its fate. It must marry poor, or marry not at all. A week or two the lad who was to be the groom would be chopping in the woods. He would spend a day or two with a team dragging to the new homesite the logs which he had cut. Then the "raising" came. Now waxing life brought us together even as the ebbing life of my Aunt Charlotte had done, in common cause.

The women brought the food. The men chopped and grunted and hurrahed. By night the heap of logs had become a house, a home. A new family, poor but free, was set, by our united effort, hustling on its way. Such our wedding gift!

We drank in the hills from springs and creeks, and the "fever" was no stranger there. Too many of us coughed our lives away. Smallpox was a dread, and diphtheria. There was the sadness of much sickness. To ease the sadness, there was the "sitting up." No sick man, woman, child was called upon to bear his cross alone. No sick one lacked for neighbors to "sit up" with him. No mother with an ailing child lacked help with the nursing and the house. We bore one another's burdens in the hills.

All we had of great value in those cabined hills was each other. Good neighbors were our wealth. The man who lacked good neighbors, or who was himself not one, was poorest of the poor, bankrupt without resource or hope. This world, my home, was neighbors, folks.

We live in cities now. The name of the family next door we hardly know. Does one need a house, he buys one, mortgaged. Is he sick, he calls a doctor. Does he need a nurse, he hires one. Does he die, heaven help his bank account! Does he need sympathy? God may give it him. We are wealthy, prosperous, now, as my happy, shouting Aunt Charlotte never was. No?

5

My world and school

I WAS LIFTED UP IN THE FIRELIGHT, still in infant dress, to see a puppy at the bottom of a barrel. He was a stranger and I was afraid of him. But not for long. We grew up together, this mongrel dog and I. He was to be my companion and bodyguard throughout my boyhood in the hills.

He found and fought the snakes, some of them copperheads, that hissed at me. The frenzied cow that took after me in the woods, head down, horns sharp and glistening, changed her mind and direction when Haze, at a leap, attached himself to her ear. He helped me gather the straying stock at milking time. No hostile neighbor dog, thanks to Haze, could come near me. Was I caught out, frightened, in the dark, there was my fearless bodyguard to reassure and lead the way for me.

Fathers, mothers, aunts, uncles, cousins make up a world which shields and shapes the plastic boy. Do not forget, meanwhile, his dog. His dog is a friendly link between the boy and the fearsome world with which he must learn to live. In the oneness of boy and dog lies the germ of a faith to be needed in his manhood years. Faith with the dog grows into faith with men.

There were the chickens as well as Haze to help with my learning. I early learned the tender care a peeping chick requires. An adolescent cockerel was a playmate. He would eat from my hand. He would nestle happily, chuckling his pleasure, in my arms.

There was the delight of outwitting the ancient hen who perversely hid her nest. The clever creature! Into the woods she'd slyly steal. There would be a great cackling soon. No hen can lay an egg and repress her song of triumph to the waiting world. Into the woods, in the direction of the cackling, we would run. No nest, no eggs! She had laid her egg in her chosen nest and from some other spot, far away, had cackled her joy and our despair.

The barnyard birds had, even in that day, a bomb suspended over them. In the woods and in the air lurked hungry hawks. When the geese let go their raucous sirens, it was for the children to rush forth with shouts and a beating of tin pans to repel the aerial aggressors. A boy, in that day, was a "civil defense" against jet carnivores.

There were the cows to hunt in the woods, then milk. Then the calves to be broken to the yoke. No boy, set to train a calf to take the yoke, could doubt the difference, plainer than your nose, between Buck and Berry, between Bill and Tobe. I learned to deal with oxen as with dogs, according to their temperament. A "herd" of cattle, all alike? There was never such a thing. Well did I learn that, herding those individualistic, contrary animals afoot on the Burcham farm! No boy, so educated by animals would ever commit the blunder, common to men in power, of thinking of mankind as the "masses." No one man was ever just like any other man.

The creatures around us, even the wild ones which we sought for food, were wards and friends of ours. We excepted, of course, the "varmints," the chicken-killing weasel, the wildcat, and in Nebraska the coyote, a creature no one respected, no one loved. To the boy in the woods the wild creatures spoke in languages all their own. We were sure that the crow, if we caught him young and split his tongue, would learn to talk. Would he? We never got around to testing the theory.

The toad was to be watched, not touched. Who handled a toad was sure, in the lore of that land, to have warts on his hands. I carefully refrained from touching any toad; and yet, what warts on my hands I had!

There was discrimination to exercise among the serpents of the rocky slopes. Beware the rattler, the copperhead. Fear not the blacksnake, the blue racer, the garter snake, the water snake. The hoopsnake, that mythical relentless creature which rolled toward you, fanged tail in mouth, ready to strike you or a tree or anything dead at a single blow, I feared as I feared a wailing witch or ghost.

Of all my untamed teachers of the wild, the birds were most alluring, enduring, dear. Here I started early to a school from which no student ever graduates. Who pursues the birds without a gun is on a trail which, like the trail of wisdom, has no end. The sun was struggling forth, low in the west, after an April rain. Out of the woods, as the sun sank in a fire of its own making, a bird voice floated. I must have been hearing birds sing all my previous seven years. Why do I remember clearly, to this day, that one time and place and song? I do not know the mystery of memory, of what it discards, of what it keeps. But from that showery evening even until now that wood thrush has been ringing in my ears, calling me forth to healthy hours in field and wood, consorting with the creatures there. In this world of mine, a friendly communion with the birds is, in ways I do not claim to understand, companionship with Life itself.

Learning, from the world around us, we all acquired—schooling, some of us had. Abe Wilson did not know "a" from "z," yet he was good as the best as farmer, woodsman, neighbor. His son, John, equally allergic to letters, grew up an able and useful member of our hill country community and later a prosperous farmer in the west.

John Poynter had reached only the Fifth Reader class in school, yet he brought hundreds, by his preaching, to the mourners' bench. If my Grandmother Shields could read, I never saw her try. What a grandmother, with her weaving, sewing, cooking, soapmaking and helping of her neighbor, she was! Abe Wilson, John Poynter and my grandmother lived passing well the lives their circumstances allowed. What angel could do more?

We had four months of school, in winter. Of education, we had twelve months a year. I was born at school to a hoe. As soon as he learned to walk, the boy in that country was on his way to be an artist with the hoe. The skills which the hoeing of corn, potatoes and beans inspired were infinite. We had learned discussions then (as now with motor cars), of the virtues of the various shapes and weights of hoes. There was joy in genius with the hoe. When the frosts put an end to the hoeing, I hung up in triumph a hoe worn thin as a crescent moon in its summer wrestling with stone and weed and sod.

From the elementary education of the hoe the boy moved up, grade by grade, to the higher education of mattock, rake, pitchfork, ax, ox-whip and saw. (The girls, inside the house and out, were growing, in their own way, too.) There were bachelors of the science of the broadax and masters of the art of the saw. My Uncle Jim was a doctor of philosophy with a little water wheel that turned out the makings of biscuits and buckwheat cakes. There were dullards, of course, who never mastered anything. In these hills of equal opportunity the number of these was small.

It helped, in all this higher education, to know how to read. We were not content with the knowledge and power that served the flesh alone. There were higher aspirations to which the printed word could mightily minister. Over the forest-clad, mist-enveloped hills brooded ever a mystery. What lay beyond the hills we might assume from what lay this side of them. But what world stretched above the hill, above the very sky? Death came often in our hills to arouse our wonderings.

My Aunt Lide, always yearning, had another mystery than these half-hid hills in mind. There was much singing of "the world over there." The guidebook to the overhanging mystery was the big Book from which John Poynter preached. To be able to read the Book was a soul-saving privilege. Furthermore, young men were going west, and writing home of the glories out there. It was desirable, not only to be able to read these letters, but also to write letters in return. Reading and writing were tools as practical as the hammer, scythe and hoe.

The four-month school term was the time for books. Children learned to read from the Book to parents who could not read themselves. The children, too, were soon able to do the family problems in financial arithmetic. Such knowledge was too obviously useful to arouse the hostility of ignorance.

With this learning went its application in the pupils' work with ox-team and ax. There was no graduating from this four-month's school and counting one's education done. Here, letters and labor worked together like your two hands with the ax. What is education but a lifetime labor, a learning and doing together without end? Life and learning linked like the two sides of a dime!

It was scanty fare, this brief schooling with the books. Was it because of that it was consumed with so fierce an appetite? Here was no compulsory school attendance law. The school bell rang. Such as desired would be there crying to be exposed to reading, writing and arithmetic. These would stay as long as the pursuit of knowledge pleased them—and no more.

Some plodded through their A B C's and on to "I see the cat" in bashful monotone and disappeared. Others ventured as far as the Fourth Reader and long division, and felt that this sufficed. It was enough to serve their mental appetites and vocational purposes. A few stormed through all the Readers, like fire through flax, to the very Fifth and Sixth. They won the spelling bees. They could sing the multiplication table forwards and backwards. They even knew the names of all the state capitals. These would in time pass from sight beyond the hills, to come to view later in all quarters of the earth as teachers, lawyers, doctors, preachers, politicians, scholars, businessmen.

There has been disputing, all through my life, as to what an education ought to be. When we agree as to what a man should be we may agree on the education of the man. Meanwhile, what passed for education in my boyhood hills, with its great school of experience and little school of books, was open opportunity, without forced feeding of the mind. It helped us help ourselves to our feet, then left us free, if so disposed and endowed, to sprout and spread our wings.

6

A new world: its men

THE WORLD TO WHICH I WAS BORN was all forested hills and knife-edged hollows. It was a world of secret shades and glades, a world, to the eye of a boy, of mystery. Of a sudden my world became an almost level, almost treeless plain where nothing could be concealed. Here the houses stood stark against the horizon, open to world and wind. A load of hay on the highway was as a mountain height. Even the stars hung lower in the sky, the better to be seen. Men who had been dwarfed by the hills towering over them, here towered, themselves, above the level plain.

Such was the change from the West Virginia hills to the prairies of the Platte. Here less was left to be imagined, more was to be seen. We had crossed our Rubicons—the Ohio, the Mississippi, the Missouri—in pursuit of our share of the beckoning West. A thin stream of the more venturesome, the first to take warning from the waning forests of the hills, had preceded us. When we arrived, my cousin Jack was at the railroad station with a spring-seated lumber wagon, our first taste of new luxury, to take us home with him.

Going West, even as lately as 1884, was not, as now, an instantaneous enterprise. We left the old home by jolting wagon on a November Sunday midnight to catch a morning train at St. Marys, nine steep and crooked miles away. Not till the fourth day and the eighth change of cars did we reach Nebraska and the village not far from Lincoln where our new world awaited us. Well enough the transition was slow! Too sudden change is death. Looking backward now, I seem to have lived longer in those four days between two worlds than in any decade afterward.

Every stretch of the thousand miles in that journey is an etching on my brain. The leveling out of the land as we passed from jagged East to rolling West; the thinning of the trees, with a corresponding widening of the fields; the countless towns!

What boy of the thinly-peopled hills could have dreamed there was so much land, so many people in the world?

The conductor of the train, my first sight of grand and awful uniformed dignity! The "train boy," proposing to sell us three flattened figs for a dime—a dime, bigger than a dollar now! The child in the Chicago bus calling its dancing oil lights johnny-jump-ups. The woman carrying her bird, like a homesick memory, in a cage along with her into the new world. Every moment an expanding exploding of my world!

We had been warned by the stay-at-homes that "a rolling stone gathereth no moss." My Aunt Becky had flung back, "a settin' hen never gets fat." However that be, milk must be churned to get butter. A terrific churning of the mind was this changing of worlds for me.

In the hills we had been of one blood as far back as Andrew Jackson's time. Thence had come our politics. Everybody but Abe Wilson, who could not read, was a Democrat. Up on the ridge, where water was scarce, we were Methodists, baptized by sprinkling. Down on McKim, where water was plentiful, they were Baptists. Our religious difference was merely an accident of geography; in spirit we were one. The new world, when I reached it, had been settled by peoples from all parts of the earth. Veterans of the Union Army had had first claim on the virgin soil. That made the new land all but unanimously Republican. This fact forced me to abandon, as my acquaintance grew, the idea to which I was born, that Republicans had horns and hoofs and forked tails. They were human, I discovered, even as Democrats. A surprise, as it ever is to all it dawns on, but not an unpleasant one.

Jim Musseter, who generously called on our first Sunday to drive us to church, was leader of the choir and, of all things, a Republican. So even a Republican could be an attractive candidate for heaven when he died! I was pained to find that the Republicans had a corresponding reluctance to concede human quality to us Democrats.

Men, I have found, are better than their opinions, their prejudices. It was not long before, in the intimate contacts of village life, both sides of us forgot who was Democrat and who Republican; and almost even who was Lutheran and who Methodist. The issue was, rather, which was a good neighbor, which not.

The shaking up of the transplanted mind by the impact of plains and politics was not all. Into this new world had come a flood of "foreigners." In Saline county one heard as much Bohemian as English speech. Germans, carrying their Lutheran church along with them, were everywhere. Some communities were Swedish and in others the Irish ruled. China was represented by its laundrymen, and we had our remnants of Pawnee, Winnebago and Sioux Indians.

The "foreigner" learned of us. We learned of him. All manner of worlds were mingled here and the melting pot simmered slow. Minds, like cement, tend to calcify if left alone. Minds so mixed and stirred together, as ours were there, how could they turn to bone, or stone?

There was here, save for a little firewood along the creeks, no timber to harvest. Here was a corn economy in place of the old oak and pine economy. For a job, we worked on the railroad, or in the quarry, or the store. The problems of this new economy were already, in the 1880's, pressing on our politics, shattering shapes to which our minds were born. A new world was minting new minds.

Cousins who stayed on in the hills have lived fruitful, happy lives. The setting hen can get fat. They found their own ways to keep awake. For the fortune that flung me from one world into another I rejoice. The rolling stone, even if it gathers no moss, does gather awakening experience, especially that of knowing many kinds of men.

Men—uncles, cousins, neighbors—had made up my world in the hills. They were scattered on their little farms, and the hills and hollows hid them. A certain dimness covered them. Now in the West I was set, homesick for cousins and woods and hills, among strangers in a flat, unshaded land. In this new world nothing stood forth to overshadow the people of it. No hollows hid them. No hills walled them away. We were gathered in a village where each man stood out, mountan or molehill, by himself.

A dozen miles south of Lincoln, new capital of the new state, and booming accordingly, an outcropping of the limestone which

underlies the prarie showed itself. This rock, thus accessible, was
needed for the foundations of the new city and for the walls of
the state prison that rose outside the town. A quarrying industry
had grown here, accordingly, giving rise to the village named
for its rocks. Thither had come from everywhere the men to
swing the picks and drive the drills and push the wheelbarrows.
Blasting powder to loosen up the ledges, and horses to pull the
scrapers in clearing away the soil above the stone, were all men
had to fortify their muscle here.

Here came Henry Miller from Germany to wrestle with the
rock. Harry Langlois came from France and Dick Andersen
was a Dane. There were Swedes, Irish, Bohemians, Welshmen,
New Englanders. Here my father found a job as quarryman, a
dollar and a half for a ten-hour day. Here were men with strange
tongues and broken English. What men they were!

I doubt if John Chrisbaum could read and write, but he was
a sledge hammer with his fists when roused, and, on his merits,
our outstanding quarryman. He grunted more than he talked.
His life of steady, heavy labor spoke for him. Bill Smith, another
example of shut-mouthed diligence, by his strength and skill as
a quarryman attracted my respect. Jim McVey, with top seniority
on the railroad section gang, was a prodigy with a shovel and a
genius at tamping ties. Dan Brown ran the eight-by-ten foot
candy store. He was the small boys' merchant prince, as quick
to supply one stick of striped candy for my impecunious penny
as a ten-cent plug of Horseshoe for a freshly-paid quarryman.

Tom Darling, the barber, was a swarthy man with a deep
scar in his cheek and, when I arrived in the village, he was wear-
ing his hair in a queue tied with a piece of string. Here must be
a story for the book I was even then planning. Tom Darling,
like so many of his neighbors, had been a soldier in the recent
war. A Confederate bullet had laid that scar on his cheek. That
was the doing, to his mind, of a devilish "rebel" Democrat. The
election of 1884 had made Grover Cleveland, a Democrat, president. Outraged at this misfortune of the country he had fought
to save, Barber Darling had sworn a most unbarberlike oath.

His head, he vowed, should be as unsheared as Samson's as
long as a degraded Democrat defiled the White House. His hair,

when I first met him, had had a year to grow. It presented no
mean pigtail even then. Before the four years were up, and the
nation redeemed with Republican Benjamin Harrison, the Dar-
lings had moved away. How long was that pigtail to be? I was
never to write the story, for I did not know its end.

Barber Tom Darling, with the courage of his conviction (call
it prejudice if you must) stands forth in my memory today, a
rebuke to my weak-backed moments, a man to count upon.

To young Fred Foster a wheelbarrow piled high with stone
was as a feather's weight. He was a Titan, flinging boulders
about with a strong man's disdain and an artist's grace. The
village doctor, Henry Clay Demaree, moved with sober dignity
among us, his quinine and calomel keeping our houses in order,
his five dollars a baby keeping our houses filled. He chewed
fine-cut tobacco, not plug, as the rougher rest of us did.

I could go on and on the full length of the village street, for
every man there was a free state in himself, a self that stands
forth in memory. For here no man or woman lived concealed.
I saw them all as fish in bowls. What I saw was food for unending confidence and sympathy. There were no perfect saints. There
were no perfect sinners. We were all born equal. We grew
according to our capacity.

Amos Warner, a farmer's son, went on from here to a
scholar's life, an eminent university economist. Emory Buckner,
the preacher's son, wrought his way through Harvard to a partnership in law with Elihu Root. Most of us, of course, flew lower.
Like the gray geese in the flock of Mother Goose, some flew east
and some flew west, but each one flew as he flew best.

One who grows up in a village and throughout his life returns
there has this rare privilege. He sees the lives of his childhood
mates from their infant beginnings to their aged ends. He can
chart the paths they have traveled, measure their triumphs and
defeats. He sees their lives clearly and he sees them whole. He
sees no two lives in the least alike.

Having had this rich experience, I could never see men as a
mass, a class, a nationality, a race. I could only see each as a world
in himself, with his need to be free, to be himself, uncoerced by
me or by any machine or man.

7

A captive and a king

DOWN ON MCKIM CREEK, in the hills, my Uncle John reigned over an empire. He was the king. My Aunt Margaret was the queen. Her two spinster sisters were the queen's helpers and companions. Two princes, sons of the family, completed the royal line.

In this kingdom there were no subjects or serfs. Mountaineers, as the motto of West Virginia goes, are always free. No man should serve, save by free exchange of service, any other man. The king, as should be the case with any proper throne, was with one exception the hardest working member of the royal family. The exception, of course, was the queen. Man worked from sun to sun. Woman's work was never done.

How long my Aunt Margaret worked I was never allowed to learn. When I woke in the morning she was working. When I went to sleep at night she was working still. Did she ever stop work to sleep? How was I to know?

Here was a kingdom in a land of liberty. Everybody had to work; but where there is no slave driver, where is the slave? The kingdom ruled by my uncle, King John, was subject to the needs which weigh on men everywhere. The king, and no less the queen and her royal sisters and the princes of the family, must eat. Kings, like other folks, need good food and plenty. Queens want less, but better, more delicate food. Young princes, of course, are happy to eat anything, just so there be enough.

There must be shelter, of course, for a king and his family. It need not be a palace of stone or brick. In the case of my Uncle John the royal habitation was of logs, with a great stone fireplace at one end and the royal couch at the rear. It was warm in winter and cool in summer, which is all even royalty should desire. With the evening firelight playing on the rafters while the king sat at leisure by the fire and the queen worked at her knitting, the

royal scene would suffice to serve a Raphael. The hills had their
winters with their snows. Warm coats and stockings and panta-
loons and skirts were a pressing necessity. Royalty must have its
robes. Could a king be subject to all these needs—house, food,
raiment—and yet be free, a king?

All these things my uncle, King John, and his queen, my
Aunt Margaret, had in sufficiency. They did not lack them. They
had no fear of lacking them. Yet they were not beholden to any
man. Why? They provided them, by their own labor. They
depended only on themselves. No monopoly, no want of money,
no strikes, could overthrow this king. With his empire of a
hundred acres he ruled his own destiny.

His palace he had built himself of logs and shingles from
his own woods. For fireplace, the stones from the bed of the creek
sufficed. Clay mixed with water served for cement. For his fuel,
his own forest, with the help of his own ax and saw, gave all
he could require.

The food? A patch of corn on the bit of bottom land; a field
of wheat on the hillslope; there was bread enough and more.
To turn the grain to flour he had only to go horseback down the
creek to the little water mill run by my Uncle Jim. For this
service my Uncle Jim took, not money, but his "toll." The king
returned, financially untroubled, his meal and flour behind him
on his horse, to his throne.

For meat there were pigs self-fattened on acorns in the woods.
There were rabbits for the princes to trap, and squirrels. There
were potatoes and turnips from the straw-lined, anti-freezing
excavation in the ground. The parsnips were more tender after
freezing. The tomatoes and fruits stood in jars on cellar shelves.
Chickens, the only heads in jeopardy in the kingdom of my
Uncle John, were plentiful. For sugar, the sorghum patch, the
maple tree. Other kingdoms might have their famines. There
were none in the empire of my Uncle John.

The robes for the royal family were the last thing to worry
such a king. This was the province of the queen. With a high
left hand she rules. The family sheep, what an humble friend of
kings! Such a shearing, carding, spinning, weaving went on!
Such dyeing with butternut, walnut and all the brightness the

women extracted from the fields and woods! After that, the
cutting, the sewing! For bedding, the feathers from their own
geese. The blankets they wove themselves.

What time for plotting against the government in those busy,
self-sufficient hills? Anyway, who wanted to plot against himself? The milk and honey, in the empire of my Uncle John, did
not flow. It had to be worked for. It was slow but it was sure.
Was there too little, they worked the harder. Was there too
much, such overplus as yields poverty in the midst of plenty
nowadays, they laid off working. They played awhile. They went
fishing in McKim.

There could be no panics, for there were no debts to pay, no
banks to fail. There was no problem of unemployment in that
realm. All worked until they had enough, then joined, for a time,
the privilege of the rich, the leisure class. With supply and demand in balance, supply in the right hand, demand in the left,
no depression could occur. Here was economic education in my
boyhood hills. Elsewhere I was to live through the devastating
panics of '93 and '29 and the minor catastrophes between. In the
light of the secure economy in the kingdom of my Uncle John
in the West Virginia hills, how silly, strange, those panics and
depressions seem!

This Uncle John, on his steep and stony soil, was subject to
no man—a king. Surely my Uncle Jim, who had moved from
his little mill on McKim to the fat black humus of the Nebraska
plains, would be yet more a king, free from the power of any
man. In the freedom of my Uncle John, my education in eco-
nomics, the way men get their wealth, began. My studies were
now to continue in the realm of my Uncle Jim.

Uncle Jim had preceded us into the West. With his little
capital he had bought a farm not far from the village where my
father was to work as a quarryman. His home sheltered us while
we were finding a place of our own to live. Here I surveyed, with
the wide eyes of a boy, the kingdom, as I supposed, of my Uncle
Jim and Aunt Lib, his queen.

I awoke, on my first morning there, to the sight of such a
store of corn, huge yellow ears, as I had never imagined, much
less seen before. It was late November. The husking was done

and the crop was in the crib. Here was a mountain of corn, a
thousand bushels or more. What wealth! The kingdom of my
Uncle John back in the hills suddenly seemed poor and mean.
Here was corn enough for mush and milk and pone for a
hundred royal families. Here was Croesus as well as king. What
could my Uncle Jim do with such a wealth of corn? Here was
a pleasant problem which my education in the empire of my
Uncle John had not prepared me for.

Half this corn, my Uncle Jim explained, he would sell for
money to buy the many things his farm did not provide. The
rest he would feed to the pigs. That would fatten enough pigs
to feed a dozen families. What would he do with the pigs he
could not eat? He would sell them, he said, to the local livestock
buyer, who would ship them to Omaha to a commission merchant there, who would sell them to the packers, who would
make them into pork to be shipped back to the merchants to be
sold to the people of the towns.

The money got for the pigs, like that for the corn, must buy
coal for the winter fire and, he hoped, clothes for the family. He
needed also one of the new harvesting machines then coming
into use. It might take the whole thousand bushels of corn just
to buy one of the new harvesters. As I questioned my Uncle Jim,
I noted a deep anxiety in his voice. A man with all this corn, all
these pigs, what could he have to worry him?

The potato crop which my Uncle Jim was ready to harvest
was to add further to my bewilderment. In the free domain of
my Uncle John, potatoes came few and small. Plant them, hoe
them, "bug" them as we might, a dozen bushels to bury beneath
the reach of frost was the best we could hope for. Yet with only
these my Uncle John felt secure. There they were to eat. What
else should they be for?

Now here in the prairie field of my Uncle Jim the potatoes
ran in rows a quarter mile in length. Uncle Jim drove his plow
down the row as fast as a horse could walk, and there in sight
the wealth of potatoes lay. It was then for such as I to gather
them up and throw them into piles to be loaded on the wagon
and hauled, the hundreds of bushels of them, to the storage bin.
Here were potatoes enough to relieve a famine in Ireland. I had

heard of the riches of the Rothschilds. The name of John D. Rockefeller even then resounded in the land. And here, right here, was my Uncle Jim with all this wealth, these potatoes for his own.

One day, late in the following winter, I met my Uncle Jim leaving, with a grave face, the office of the local buyer and shipper of such produce as farmers had to sell. How had he come out with the potatoes I had helped him harvest? His reward had been rich, of course? He had just been offered ten cents a bushel for his crop, he said, and was hoping for fifteen. At less than that the crop would not pay for the seed from which it grew. His corn? He had sold some at fifteen cents a bushel. The rest he was burning in the heating stove at home. At the price offered him, corn for fuel was cheaper than coal.

This was my introduction to the baffling problem of our modern machine age economy. My Uncle John, being his own market for his own product, was, albeit poor, a king. My Uncle Jim, his product in other hands and mouths, was producing richly, yet he was dependent, poor. Here was that stubborn paradox, poverty in the presence of plenty—poverty produced by plenty!

My Uncle Jim with his machinery and his mellow soil was pouring forth floods of food. Because of his plenty, the price was so small he was hard pressed to pay taxes and the interest on the mortgage, say nothing of buying the coal and clothes and machines the farm must have. Uncle John, in his rocky hills, was producing little, but he had that little securely for himself. He was free, a king. If his was a hand-to-mouth economy, the hand and mouth were both his own. He must work hard, but the product of his labor was his own.

The hand of Uncle Jim produced abundantly, but between his hand and his mouth stood a line of other hands and mouths. So little, at the end of that circuit, came back to my Uncle Jim!

As Uncle Jim emptied his cellar of the decaying potatoes he could not sell, a low rumbling on the prairies was rising to a roar. The farmers were asking why, as their corn and meat went from hand to hand to market and back again, so much was withheld from them. They talked of grain trusts and meat trusts and rail-

road monopolies and "greedy middlemen." Their revolt sparked
the movement that was to make famous such names as Bryan,
"Teddy" Roosevelt, Woodrow Wilson, La Follette, "FDR,"
suppliers of the slogans of half a century of politics—"Square
Deal," "New Deal," "Fair Deal."

Was our economy a gamble, that its issues should thus be
couched in gambling terms? For my Uncle Jim it surely was.
In the corn belt, as the old century aged, the question would not
down. Why should the plenty which my Uncle Jim produced
lead him into insecurity, while the little of my Uncle John found
him safe, a king? I was to find this question central in the
economy and the politics of all my life to come.

8

The rockpile: a dying age

MY NEW WORLD, in 1887, was fast filling up. A new hotel, the Lincoln, full six stories high, was to be built to help house the statesmen converging on the capital. For its foundations, a train-load of concrete would be required. At Roca we had the stone. After quarrying it must be broken up by hand. This was work boys could do. The new hotel, like other needs of the booming capital, ushered in, for the boys of the village, a golden age.

For making a living and a life, the perfect world, it has seemed to me, would be a place where work was always waiting, and where men could work as pleased them, each to have the fruits, much or little, of such labor as he performed. There each would determine his own wealth. If one chose to study in poverty rather than exhaust himself with work, that would be his privilege. His hunger could be on his own head. Here, with all riches earned and no poverty unearned, would be a golden age.

The practical obstacles to this perfection I must admit. My uncle, King John, in his empire in the hills, came close to it; but his Utopia missed the gains from division of labor and farm machinery, a serious lack. We wrestle with the problem, accordingly, at the level of our more complicated age. That wrestling, as our way of living goes, makes most of the turmoil of our time.

But with all this stone to shatter in the quarries the golden age for a twelve-year-old boy had dawned. The small boy borrowed the family hammer. He betook him, in the early morning, to the quarry a mile away. He preempted, on the rocky floor, a space for his activity. A circle a dozen feet in diameter would hold, heaped up, a carload of the output of his enterprise. A friendly quarry hand would dump here wheelbarrow loads of spalls, splinters of rocks, by-product of the quarrying, too small for building stone. This was the raw material for the new enterprise.

Now, with his hammer in hand and a gunny sack to sit on, the boy was in business for himself. Every cubic yard of concrete hammered out made thirty-five cents for the young business-man. How big is a cubic yard? Ray's *Arithmetic*, our school authority, had one idea of a cubic yard. The boy who had ham-mered out a cubic yard of concrete knew better. A cubic yard was slightly smaller than a good-sized house.

There we sat, the summer day through, hammering out our rising pyramids of broken stone. Our rattling hammers added their staccato to the song of the grasshoppers in the fields around. We could make our day as short or long as pleased us. But we were working for ourselves, independent businessmen. Our pride and our pockets together dictated the same ten-hour day as the men around us served. At the end of the day, the boy of twelve, if he flagged not on the job, might have to his credit a mountain of two cubic yards of concrete. He had earned a fabulous seventy cents that day.

As we worked, with the left hand we fed the unbroken stone to the hammer in the right. From constant gripping of the handle of the hammer, the blistered flesh of the palm would be crowded down upon the fingers, making a stiff and hooked hand. To this day I cannot quite straighten the fingers of my right hand.

With this constant handling of the stone, the tips of the fingers of the left hand would sometimes wear through to the quick and bleed. We stained with our blood the product of our toil. To this day, when I visit Lincoln, I live at the hotel which my labor helped to build. I feel a proprietary interest there. Is not my very life blood built into the foundation of the place?

Every tow-headed boy like me was encouraged, in those days, to consider himself a candidate for President. The White House, like the stone quarry, was a yawning opportunity. From rockpile to President! What a tale! I laid up in my heart the marks of these bleeding fingers on the bludgeoned rock against the day when they might wring out a million tearful votes. So rise, to melt like desert snows, our boyhood dreams!

Here on our rockpiles the unobstructed sun, each ray of it, smote us twice. There was the direct stroke from above, then its rebound from the bare stone walls around. We did not mind.

We were working, growing, prospering. The hot sun of summer meant warm coats in winter. Warm coats are warmer when you have warmed yourself earning them. The rockpile is, in tradition, a place for criminals. It was the making of free men here.

Unskilled labor? There is no such thing. There is skill in everything done well. There was a way with easy hammer strokes to chip a rock till it seemed almost to dissolve into concrete by itself. There was a way to beat a rock with so little sense you only beat yourself. Bill Foster, no stronger than the rest of us, could pile up more concrete in a day than any of us. Even I, no genius, attained such joy in mastering a rock as one greater might take in the building of a state.

The dignity of labor! Walking home with emptied dinner pail from my first day's work on the rockpile, I was lordlier than Napoleon Bonaparte, taller than Alexander the Great, almost the equal of grizzled John Chrisbaum, master quarryman, walking in state beside me there.

Through the summer of 1887 the golden age in the Nebraska stone quarry went gloriously. There was work for all. There was a business of his own for every boy with the will to work—work on the rockpile that meant shoes and skates and peanut bars and the swelled up chest that goes with well-earned cash in hand.

The winter came. We went back to school with the next year in mind. Spring approached. We looked to our hammers. Some of us had hammers, supposed to be specially potent, made to order by our talented blacksmith, Casper Dice.

We tensed our biceps and planned, the minute the frost left the ground and rock ledges, for rich and joyous contributions to the world's crushed rock supply. As we waited for that happy day there came from the city, the market for our stone, a horrifying tale. Heartless men up there were building a machine, steam-powered, that could crush more concrete in a minute than a boy with his hammer could break in a day.

My golden age was ended. I was a victim at the tender age of thirteen of technological unemployment. My education on the rockpile, brief but permanent, was done. I had seen one way of getting a living dissolve in the West Virginia hills. We had met, by flight to the new world, the West, the crisis this entailed.

Now here I was again undone by shifting circumstances. Was keeping alive to depend everywhere and forever on quickness to find new footing as the world moved under us?

In my school geography was a picture of a lumberjack riding floating logs in a raging river, keeping himself alive by leaping, as the changing flow required, from spinning log to log. So life was to be like that! That, indeed, as the ensuing decades of dizzy change have proved, was what life was to be.

My concrete breaking job was gone, but, given some time to grow, I could still be a quarryman. I had only to wait till I was big as John Chrisbaum, our most eminent quarryman. Opportunity would not wait. Before I could qualify, by age and weight, as a quarryman, the quarry was no more. The quarry began where the rock showed shallow at the bottom of a slope. That stone exhausted, the working moved back into the slope, the going growing deeper at every move. At some point, the value of the rock would no longer pay the cost of stripping away the increasing earth above it. Then the quarrying must cease. On this course, the peak of the Roca quarries had passed when we arrived in 1884. The quarry south of town had been abandoned even before we came. The quarry to the north was going well but its decline was on the way.

As the work slowed down, men drifted away in search of other work. Big Fred Foster found a job in a brickyard near the city. John Berry went wandering after Alaska gold. My cousins, Jack and Charley, went on west, the one to Washington, the other to Idaho. Casper Dice, the blacksmith, turned to the breeding of light Brahma chickens. John Chrisbaum, a war veteran, could settle back on his pension as a veteran—eight dollars a month, the lucky man!

The most unusual course was taken by my Uncle Evans. While others went on to the farther West, he turned backward with my Aunt Lide to live out his days in the hills whence he had come.

My father, his world for the second time fallen from under him, turned farmer and so lived out his days. The farm, surely, is one thing that can not slip from under you. Yet nowhere, in my length of years, has there been more change, more need to watch one's step, than on the fleeting farm—the riches-to-rags, the rags-to-riches farm.

The village itself, having lost its living, must find new footing or decay. Many a "ghost town" has emerged from the changes of these years of mine. Our village shrank a bit. The Lutheran church was moved away. The Foster home vanished from its hill. The rest of the village, with farmer support, dreamed on. Then the cars and the pavements came. It was only twenty minutes, on one's own power, to the towering new capitol. The stricken home of the dead industry of my boyhood goes to meet, as a "suburb," today's exploding city a dozen miles away.

A vagrant photographer took, in the year of my golden age, a picture of my school, the whole thirty-two of us. I can trace, in memory, the lives from beginning to end of every one of us. The sixteen girls married and lived, as far as I have heard, happy ever afterward. The boys, from little Frank Swarts to big Elmo Hartz, scattered everywhere. Not one was to spend his life in the village where he had his education on the rockpile and in the school. Each one, here set on his own nimble feet, has gone the distance and reached the height to which his tastes and talents entitled him. The gift of freedom and opportunity brought each of us all he had a right to ask.

That steam-powered concrete crusher ended, in 1888, my golden age, my rockpile paradise. Older men, if they chose, could move to the city and live by feeding the machine that had stopped the flow of food to me. For a thirteen-year-old there was a better choice. The farmers needed help in harvest time. A-farming I would go.

John Wilson, the year-'round hired man on the Burcham farm, could not read or write but he could teach. He taught me farming from the handling of a pitchfork to the harnessing of a horse, the capping of a grain shock, the steering of a plow. He taught, as good teaching does, by instruction, example and practice.

A notion was current in those days, well exploded now, that "any fool can farm." If you weren't good for anything else, you could farm. Farming was then, in fact, even as now, a highly skilled activity. There are right and wrong ways of handling a pitchfork, as of swinging a baseball bat, or preaching a sermon, or running a steamboat line.

They were making fun, in those days, of the schools for farmers then growing in the West. For me, John Wilson was an agricultural college in himself. What he knew about plowing and planting he taught me well. One can farm now, of course, without touching a pitchfork or harnessing a horse. The facts of farming, like the facts of pharmacy and of most other things, have changed. I would not know now how to run a farm. Yet the best that I learned from John Wilson on the Burcham farm in the summer of 1888 stands unchanged. Can any man's education be complete without a course of study on a farm?

Between the ten-hour day in the quarry and the working hours on the farm a broad gulf lay. The quarryman could doze till seven. The farmer was up and going at half past four or five. His morning chores were done, his breakfast eaten, and he in the field at six. The happy quarryman was done at six—no evening chores or anything. The farmer, in the rushing summer time, was in the field till sundown. After that, the chores.

The summer I was fifteen I worked on the farm of Marshall Stein, a good and kindly man. A terrific worker, he was out in the morning at four, but he let me sleep, out of the goodness of his heart, a half hour more. My noon hour rest was spent in pumping water for the cows. I was nearly always through my chores and ready for bed by a July nightfall, say nine o'clock. Putting the wheat in the shock and getting the corn laid by was a labor to be done when the time was ripe. We worked under the lash of pressing haste. There would be time to sleep when winter came.

Who was the worse for my seventeen-hour work day on the farm? It was all in the open air, under the open sky. How hurt oneself living under the sky, breathing the free air?

The hum of a sweetly scouring plow as I followed it afoot was not unlike, for music, the purr of the engine lightly spinning your motor car. The skill in mastering, with my two-horse plow, the weeds among the corn was a joy to assuage my weariness. No game boys play before cheering crowds today employs a finer art than that of the farm hand pitching sheaves of grain to the man who built the stack. To make the sheaves turn in the air and fall, butt and head just where they ought to lie, was the skill of the Indian with his spinning tomahawk.

Most of my work on the farm was done in the furrow or in the corn rows all alone. The work was the least important consumer of my time. My body put in hours there working for Marshall Stein. My mind, all the while, was mine to do with as I pleased. Was it fair to take pay from Marshall Stein when I was really working for myself? He would get only the corn I plowed. I was getting more—the piping meadowlark, the blue of the sky, the whispering of the corn blades, the long blue distance, and all the dreams such sounds and scenes provoke in a furrow-plodding boy. I have envied men who make their living with their hands, leaving the mind, the best part of them, free, as did my labor in the fields. No man, I saw, could be enslaved whose mind was free. No man could be free whose mind some power had enslaved.

Epochal events were happening on those early summer mornings of which few folk not farmers could have dreamed. Dawn, if only we were awake to see, is fraught with mystery, with majesty. A world is being born. The chick emerging from its egg has no more shell-shattering experience than the farm boy sent forth to bring up the cows from the pasture as the east is reddening and the morning star turns dim. I wonder no more at our dearth of poets and prophets now, seeing that farmers, emancipated by their machines, no longer get up in time to witness, each summer morning, the birth of a new heaven, a new earth.

Why then was I to leave the farm for a labor which leaves the body free and claims the last ounce of energy of the mind? Does one choose his occupation, or does it choose him?

9

An opulent poverty

MONROE MUSSETTER, fourteen, wore an overcoat to church. It was the first boy's overcoat I had ever seen. It had slantwise breast pockets, the easier to warm his hands. The clearness of my memory of this sartorial luxury tells me how deeply I was moved by it. For myself, I was not to own an overcoat till I earned one, price, ten dollars, teaching school.

Mon's brother, Ozzy, brought store-bought gingersnaps for his school lunch, another sign of wealth. The two Swarts boys, sons of the Burlington section boss, wore overshoes. Their father's year-round pay of forty-five dollars a month made this easily possible.

The rest of us said among ourselves what a nuisance it would be to wear overcoats and overshoes. *Our* feet would be the colder when we took off our overshoes to put on our skates! As to the overcoat, whoever could not run fast enough to keep warm without one, what was the matter with him anyway? If we secretly envied Mon with his overcoat and Frank and Charley with their overshoes, our lack could cause us no corroding unhappiness. Our brothers in austerity were too numerous to allow of jealousy. We were too young to be unhappy anyway.

W. E. Keys, the owner of the quarry, lived in the big stone house on the hill. W. W. Dunham, postmaster after the Democrats won in '84, had a house of six rooms, two stories, in the middle of the town. From these palaces the housing ranged downward to the one upstairs room, sixteen feet square, in which my family of five lived our first Roca winter, rental, two dollars a month.

All but the big house were wood, with chimneys to serve the stoves. Water came from wells as convenient to the back door as possible. The toilet facilities occupied the most distant rear corner of the lot. The house my father was able, after a few years, to own, contained a cellar and four small rooms. From the one-room log cabin in the hills, that was truly a rise in the world. A full three hundred dollars that house and lot cost.

The men who worked as railroad section hands earned thirty dollars a month through a nine-month year. The men who worked in the quarries were paid, through about as many months, from a dollar and a half to two dollars a day. If no rain stopped the work, one might get in a "ringer"—a six-day, sixty-hour week. That meant from nine to twelve dollars a week maximum. Only the ablest quarrymen received the top two dollars a day.

The resident Methodist minister was paid four hundred and fifty dollars a year, with three other churches in his circuit to join in this support. The principal of our two-room school received fifty-five dollars a month for a nine-month year. His assistant in the primary grades, a Miss Anna Dunham, had forty dollars for her services. What Dr. Demaree, life-long physician to the place, was able to earn he never said. He died far from rich, at least. The keeper of the village store, what was his fortune? A sober story here.

Sam Frankfurter, when we came, had the dry goods and groceries. Most of what the people earned went through his hands. First thing I knew, Sam was out and Theo. Bendlage in. I worked with Sam in the hayfield afterward—a wonderful builder of a stack was he. He needed the dollar a day he earned, and he earned his dollar and more. Merchant Bendlage was a hustler and seemed to be prospering. First thing we knew, he, too, was gone and another was dispensing dry goods and groceries in his place. So in and out our merchant princes went.

I cannot prove the cause of this merchant mortality. I can only repeat the gossip which went around. These merchants, hard as they tried to be cold, sound businessmen, had hearts in their breasts. In November, when the quarries shut down for the winter, the grasshoppers and the ants among us stood revealed. The provident would skimp through the payless winter on dollars saved from their summer's toil. The grasshopper had sung through the summer paying the bills of the year before. Now here was another winter, and what was he to eat? Who but the storekeeper, trusting to next summer's pay, could see to that?

The storekeeper, bless his heart, faced up to it. But suppose no job next summer could be found. The merchant was the community's "community chest." He assumed that risk. The quarries faded. The jobs failed. What of the merchant, then?

Men then, even as now, had a way of eating next year's bread today. The modern merchant has learned to meet that system with solvency to himself, if not to his customer. Not so in our village seventy years ago. Down and out, in swift succession, our little merchants went.

In the whole village there was but one store-bought coasting sled, that of the little boy in the big stone house on the hill. There was one proud lad, son of the owner of the livery stable, who bought his candy at Dan Brown's by the nickel's worth. The rest of us "broke" our nickels and plunged by the pennyworth. That rich boy spoke out tauntingly before the crowd one night in old Dan's little store when I was sweetening my tooth to the tune of a full cent's worth. Why didn't I spend my big change first, he loudly asked.

I sank through the floor for shame. Here's the storybook sequel to that incident which moralizing McGuffey of the *Readers*, I suspect, would have doted upon. Forty years later I was foreman of a grand jury which was called upon to indict, for some underworld offense, the man into whom this boy had grown. He was the only one of my boyhood mates who went to the bad, as far as I can say. Was Harry with his nickels too rich for his own good?

We were not in the least unhappy in our equal poverty, there on the struggling plains. How little it takes to be enough, ask any of those boys without overcoats or overshoes or store sleds of seventy years ago. But our life, there in the village on the plain, was more than meat. We had our books.

Just before I got there, Henry Grimm had taught the village school and left for other fields. While there he had managed to put together a school library of a hundred and fifty books. The Children of Israel fought their way from the desert into a land flowing with milk and honey. I emerged from the West Virginia hills into a Nebraska flowing with books—the books inherited from the efforts of Henry Grimm.

Henry Grimm lived on with no great distinction for half a century. He died in an uphill struggle to make a living on a stingy farm. His passing was little noted; but in one boy's mind stands a monument, miles high, to him. When I think of Nathaniel Hawthorne and his hero tales, I think of Henry Grimm. Washington Irving and Ichabod Crane and Henry Grimm are all one name to me. William H. Prescott wrote *The Conquest of Mexico*, but Henry Grimm put the story in my hands.

One hundred and fifty books! I had not dreamed there were so many in the world. We had Bibles and hymn books in the hills. (So few of the latter the leader of the singing in church had to "line" the hymns.) We had, in my home, besides the Bible, a book of travels in the Holy Land. These, with the McGuffey *Readers* and Ray's *Arithmetic* used in school were the only books that I had ever seen.

For lack, I suppose, of lighter reading, I had read the Bible through at about the age of eight. The book of travel I had read, at least in the lighter parts, repeatedly. The McGuffey *Readers*, First to Fifth, I knew by heart. There had been the limit of my literary opportunities. A few things called paper backs had begun to circulate from hand to hand in the hills, but furtively. Tales of bloody scalpings and amorous wooings and inspired sleuthings were frowned upon by the pious, the serious.

As far as my known world of books extended, at the age of nine, I was an Alexander The Great. All of the world, my two books, was underneath my feet. No more worlds to conquer! Then to find, here in the West, this undreamed-of wealth! As the famished wanderer in the desert is supposed to plunge into the waters of the pool he at last comes upon, so I into these books.

In newspapers and magazines now I find talk of a puzzling problem which parents face. How persuade a boy to eat his breakfast, eat his supper, eat his lunch? No boy, in all my young experience, ever turned up his nose at anything to eat. Food was too limited, too hard to get, thus to be despised. We raced for the table, and if, as too often happened, the places were all claimed by the elders and a second table had to wait, the hungry woe of it!

I found myself as hungry for *Hans Brinker And His Silver Skates* as ever I had been for apples when turnips were all I had. I had been so starved for books I could pleasantly consume *Pizzaro's Conquest of Peru*. I even dared the profundities of *Sartor Resartus* and *In Memoriam*.

Today, to my amazement, I see youths in school reading *Silas Marner* and *Nicholas Nickleby* and *The Last Days of Pompeii* protestingly as a weary drudgery. In school this is "required" of them. Spading the garden under father's orders and reading *The Scottish Chiefs* by command of the curriculum are an equal drudgery to them. "Required" reading! Must a duck be forced to swim? O the times! O the manners! We must force the children to eat their breakfast, then force them to feed their brain! Such effect from a surfeit of bread! Such from a surfeit of books!

I was to learn, through many a decade to come, how evil are both too little and too much. They are the Scylla and Charybdis, warning us to keep the strait and narrow middle way.

I was myself to pay a lifelong penalty for the too much to which I was tempted by Henry Grimm's books and the other books yet to come. My greed for books grew by what it fed upon. After the books bestowed by Henry Grimm came others, not always of much worth. A book in hand, I would hide away in a treetop and follow from morning to night the fortunes of whatever two-gun man or imperiled lady the volume might portray.

One day a pain shot through my head. I was trapped into spectacles, a humiliation, in that day, for any boy. From that time on, a life with its reading restrained and often banned by weary, rebellious eyes!

To enrich our poverty we had our books. Nor was this the limit of our wealth. One more recourse and comfort was at hand.

The north wind blew unhindered, cold, across the open plain. Our houses here were of thin-sawn boards, not the warm logs left in the hills. When the Aunt Lide here must have a fire, no ax, no woodpile beckoned her. She must go off to town for coal. To purchase coal took cash. Where was the cash? There were still, on the prairie, buffalo chips to gather up and burn.

I myself have gone afield to gather cornstalks for the kitchen fire.
We twisted wisps of hay in knots and made that do for fire.
For fuel we even bundled the tall weeds from the sloughs.

To the pioneer here the gap between little and nothing was
always thin. This world, even this new world, was no secure
abiding place. I had hardly set foot on Nebraska sod when we
were going nightly to the little prairie church. There, still seeking
gold, we sang a hymn which went about like this:

> *My Father is rich in houses and lands,*
> *He holdeth the wealth of the world in his hands;*
> *Of rubies and diamonds, of silver and gold,*
> *His coffers are full; he has riches untold.*

The new world, windy and cold in winter and in summer
hot and dry, was still no heaven. Prospect of riches "over there"
helped to make this new world do. Here was only a pausing
place. This was not "home." Both poor and rich, as I watch the
world go by, I have seen peering beyond this world for something deeply desired but by this world denied. If this is a "wilderness of woe," something within suggests goodness, a justice, in
a final accounting farther on.

All this at the revival meetings we were assured anew. The
poor, as long ago we have been told, receive such news gladly.
It is grasped by "babes and sucklings" even if not by the wise.
The poor, despairing of this world's wealth, might more easily
turn to the subtler gold of another shore. The rich man, meanwhile, has an experience all his own to call him, fat as his world
is, to a better world beyond, within. He finds to his dismay that
wealth in this world is not the heaven he was yearning for. Riches
in pocket allay no poverty in the heart. He sees, like any pauper,
"This world is not my home."

Where, then, is his home? In the end we find him at the
same "mourners' bench" where the weary and heavy laden of
the hills and prairies lay their burdens down. My shouting Aunt
Charlotte, rejoicing with empty hands upraised toward the heav-
en opening above her, was one with the quiet rich man, putting
forth his gold in all good works, finding that by giving, not alone
by getting, is his real home attained.

Dennis Jones, the well digger of my Nebraska village, was known for his sudden wrath. A good man unaroused, he was furious when mad. He had badly beaten one man who had carelessly offended him.

One raw March day I was helping Jones wall up a well. My work was to fill with rocks for the wall a bucket to be let down by a windlass, to where, standing on a plank laid from wall to wall, Jones worked. Carelessly I loaded a bucket unevenly. As it swung out over the well a rock slid off and hurtled downward. It struck and broke the plank below on which Jones stood. Down into the cold, though happily not deep, water of the well went Jones.

I was terrified. If Jones survived, surely in his wrath he would murder me. To my amazed delight he climbed out, laughing, praising the Lord. There had been a revival at the church. Jones had "got religion." He was "saved,"—and so, it turned out, was I! Ah, it made saints of men, however briefly, this glimpse of their final home.

But the Eighties turned into the Nineties and another mood was coming over us on the plains. Darwin had reached the West. The debate of the decade, painful but inescapable, the evolution question, raged. Before our winter literary society I can still hear Teacher Tom Davidson singing to loud applause a ballad with the refrain:

A man is a monkey, minus the tail:
That's not what I think, do you?

10

The great debate

GEORGE AND HIS COUSIN FRANK came dancing down the sidewalk singing a skeptic song. The refrain:

> *He robbed all his Methodist breth-er-en*
> *And skipped to Canada.*

A cloud had risen to dim, in the Nineties, our prairie sky. On the heels of Charles Darwin with his evolution had come the eloquent agnostic, Robert G. Ingersoll. Before large crowds he was cutting at the roots, as in terror we supposed, of our faith in that other world. At his heels came the village "infidel," scoffing at the story of Jonah and the whale, probing the rents in the armor of piety.

A member of our community known for the eloquence of his street corner prayers had failed in business. He had fled, leaving behind him trusting brethren to rue their endorsements of his promissory notes. To him was due the glee of these sitters in the seat of the scornful as they pranced down the street. The failings of the pious, the hypocrisies of "scribes and Pharisees," what weapons for the ungodly they do supply!

The display in a Brooklyn court of the private frailties of the pulpit idol of the day had but lately fed the skeptic fire and made the judicious grieve. Doubt had sprung to the saddle. Faith was on the floor. Was faith to be counted out? Who could be sure?

Darwin with his *Origin of Species* had struck, as it seemed to us, at the very foundation of our world. The very story of creation had been assailed. If the Book were wrong here, how be sure it is right anywhere?

We had been preoccupied with the saving of our souls. What now if there be no soul to save? The assault brought sadness, suffering. If the attack was furious, the defense was desperate.

As the debate went on, brother rose against brother, husband against wife, neighbor against neighbor. That decade is now called the "Gay Nineties." This aspect of the Nineties was deathly serious. Our eternal destiny was at stake. The scene was anything but gay.

Long and bitterly we raged. When one of my mother's valued boarders, John Gilgallon, the station agent, gave vent in my tender presence to some scoffing skepticism, my gentle father warned him sternly to hold his tongue. So short was our tolerance.

I, myself, was troubled by Jonah, that gently satirical tale. My sense of humor had not then been granted scope with sacred things. When my boyhood friend, brilliant Rob Haile, went over to the enemy, I was thunderstruck. Was the world which my Aunt Lide had invoked so soulfully only a wishful dream, now in the light of science to be dissolved?

Not being learned, there on the prairie, in ancient history, we did not know how old this issue, in its essence, was. How many such issues had been fought and never ended—that we did not know. Our all, we thought, was here to be saved, or lost. What underlies the life we live? What is its nature, what its demands? What is our proper aim and destiny? What time or place or arguing can end such irrepressible questioning?

We were fighting one battle of an eternal war. We did not know that with this battle lost, the war would yet go on. For the truth, whatever it may be, is truth and cannot be destroyed. It stands unchanged by our chattering, unaltered by our arguments.

Happily for our foolishness, arguing wears itself out at last. A peace of exhaustion comes. Reason dares show its face again. So it occurred with us. In time the enemies our quarreling had made went happily riding together on the new bicycles which were not to compete, for interest, with the old theology. I encountered, meanwhile, Ralph Waldo Emerson, Thomas Jefferson, Walt Whitman, Henry D. Thoreau. I found in them a faith which shamed my own. To my discomfiture I learned that in their day each of these had been assailed by such misunderstanding men as I as horrid infidels. As always when old opinions are challenged and new facts come forth and new theories are pressed, it was a painful time. Yet out of such proddings we were stirred to better thinking, fairer minds. How vain had been our angry, egotistical arguings!

Years later I was feebly trying to put the fruit of that old debate into a word for the comfort of my worried neighbor, William J. Bryan. Mr. Bryan, long after the evolution war had waned, was still standing in horror at the evolution idea of men's origin. The Scriptures had said we came from the "dust of the ground." Now men were saying we came from lower animals. Whether of mud or monkey born, we are what we are now, I said. Quieting down, we found ourselves much closer together than, in the heat of the debate, we had pushed each other apart. The onetime "infidel" came sociably to the church. He and the minister met amiably when they came together at the post office.

And when the tuberculosis rampant in that day carried my friend Rob Haile all too soon away, Minister J. W. Embree, who had once despaired of his soul, ushered him, in a tender funeral eulogy to his purity of heart and integrity of mind, plump into paradise. So much sweeter than our heads with their proud opinions are the tested hearts of us!

11

At school

HARVE HAMILTON had sat down beside me and pointed with his pencil to a figure in a book. He said "a." In a husky voice, mark of an overwhelming awe, I said "a" after him. He pointed to the next figure and said "b." I said "b." So my first meeting with a teacher, my first day in school.

Harve Hamilton taught our four-months term of school and moved on. He was to spend his life teaching other boys their ABC's. It was sixty years before I caught up with him again. He had retired from labor and was waiting at home for his final bell to ring. I had gone far to see him. What pupil can forget a teacher who ministered kindly to him in school? Harve Hamilton, under whose pencil-pointing hundreds of bashful boys had droned their "a" and "b," even remembered me! Teachers have long memories.

In those days of ungraded schools, teacher and pupil lived together the school day through. How well they came to know each other, how deeply each was moved by the other, let my memory of Harve Hamilton and his memory of me attest. Any boy of that day could write a book on "Teachers I Have Met." Any teacher could write volumes on "Pupils I Have Known."

The big boys, on the last day of school, locked Harve Hamilton out to make him "treat." It was good, clean fun, a habit in those days, and at the end the teacher delivered a farewell address that brought tears even to big-boy eyes. Who could live four months in the schoolroom with a friendly teacher and not love him at the end?

Harve Hamilton went away. Our schooling in the work of woods and fields went on through spring, summer, fall. Then Rachel Rymer came. Under roof with school again. She was a wisp of a girl in 1881. She was a wisp of a woman when I went to see her fifty years afterward. Through all the intervening years this "old maid" had been mothering the ABC-seeking boys and girls of her West Virginia hills. Now her mothering days were done and the children she had mothered were happily mothering her. They were seeing that she lacked for nothing as she, like Harve Hamilton, awaited the final bell.

They looked out for her even as she had looked out for us. As when, on a Monday morning, she had placed in my hand a gift, the McGuffey's Fifth Reader she thought I was ready for, which my family lacked the ninety-eight cents to buy. That book, well worn, is my prized possession still. Not that I need anything visible to keep green the memory of that Rachel Rymer from whom my McGuffey came.

Next thing I know, I am in Nebraska, with its nine-months term of school, its textbooks free, and Henry Grimm's library waiting on the shelves. The settlers on the plains were hardly less poor than the people left behind in the hills. Something, the mere change, perhaps, increased their educational appetite. The new states leaped quickly to the front in support of their public schools. With its first breath as a state, Nebraska set up its university. The taxes for schools which the people imposed upon themselves were by far the largest item in their tax receipts.

The village of Roca maintained a two-room school. The teachers were always leaders in all upward activities. Only the local minister had a higher rank. Of the permanent power of Henry Grimm, founder of the school library, I have already told. Steps up a ladder, the teachers who followed him are, to me.

Soon after we entered our one-room home in the autumn of 1885, J. M. Priest, my teacher, called with an offering. Would we like his copies of *The Youth's Companion* after he and his wife were through with them? The weekly *Youth's Companion* was the Olympus of literature for the young folk of that day. We looked up to it. We adored it. It was the attainment of a lifetime ambition when, many years afterward, the *Companion* accepted, paid fifty dollars for, and printed a story which I wrote. Was it my fault that soon thereafter its existence ceased?

From William Jackson, next in line, I learned something of grammar and the dissecting of sentences. What counts with me now is his quietness, reverence, gentleness. However I lack those virtues in myself, I learned to prize them in others, thanks to

him. Tom Davidson, coming next, scoffed me out of my ambition
to follow John Chrisbaum as an inspired quarryman. Came then
soft-spirited, firm-willed Anna Ord, to push me in the direction
of a teacher's certificate. She precipitated me in 1891, aged sixteen, into a hilltop school in a neighboring county, with a score
of Bohemian children of immigrant parentage to guide to careers
as Americans.

If our teachers knew what power, all unconsciously, they are
exerting on their children's lives, they would be surprised, inspired and awed. If children knew the debt they owe to their
teachers there would never be pedestals enough to go around.
The schoolhouse door, in that prairie world of seventy years ago,
swung wide, not to the pupil only, but to the teacher, too. The
teachers easy-got estate was young ambition's stepping stone.
It was a place to take off from for wherever you were to go.

I turned up for school, from force of habit, in the year I
turned fifteen. Anna Ord seemed worried. What was I there for?
What was there for me to do? There was no graduating, in those
days, from the public school. You went to school till you were
tired of it, or grew so big you were ashamed of it. Then you
stayed away and went rabbit hunting or looking for a job.

The teacher's perplexity was matched by my surprise. I had
taken for granted I would go to school till something else turned
up. What else was I to do? She pointed out that my Swinton's
Grammar was worn out. I had long known Webster's Fifth
Reader well by heart. Barnes' United States History was no news
any more to me. No teacher I have ever known has had the heart
to turn a boy away. Anna Ord was true to her kind. The next
day as I sat idle in my seat in school she showered upon me an
armful of her own books.

The largest was a textbook on psychology. Another concerned
entomology, a live subject in a grasshopper-ridden state. There
was a treatise on the sentence method of teaching reading, where
you saw your cat at a glance, not a droning word or letter at a
time. There was "Page on Teaching," a book which placed the
proper teacher a little lower than the angels, but not much. She
had quite made up her mind, Anna Ord explained, to make a
teacher of me.

Teaching would be easier, I mistakenly supposed, than working in a quarry. The hours would be shorter, another error, than on the farm. Anna Ord's idea looked good. Why not?

In those days the transition from pupil to teacher was easy, swift. Prove you could spell, prove you could read and do simple things in arithmetic, and a certificate from the county superintendent would qualify you to teach. Now you could teach, provided you could find a school to teach. That was a matter between you and any of a hundred or two independent district school boards of the county granting your certificate.

All that year Anna Ord held me to my Psychology, my "Page on Teaching" and all the rest. I learned that even in grashoppers there is something to admire—the varied colors of their wings, once you have stretched them out. I had seen billions of grasshoppers and had never looked at one.

The school year passed and I was ready for the plunge. My county of Lancaster was overrun with students seeking teaching jobs to carry them through the university. It could afford to be particular. It would not accept a teacher less than eighteen years old. I was only sixteen. Over in Saline county I registered for the summer teachers' institute, and no one asked my age. I was wrestling with the examination in arithmetic, my weakest point, when W. C. Farrand, the county superintendent, called me to meet a solid looking farmer in his office. It was H. Vilda, director of District Number Four, looking for a teacher. He did not ask my age. What would I think of forty dollars a month? I was prepared to jump at anything. In my excitement I said I didn't think I would be worth more than thirty-seven fifty. He conceded the point. We signed a contract, eight months' school at a salary only a bit below the wages of Frank Swarts, the august Roca section boss. O, land of opportunity, land of liberty!

No occupation has more completely changed in my time than that of teaching school. Teaching, in the days of the little red brick schoolhouse, was not a profession. It was a stepping stone, a pausing place for youth poised for flights to other spheres. Half the students in the university came on their earnings from teaching school. The teachers of one day were the lawyers, politicians, editors, doctors of the next. The best spellers among my schoolmates became the teachers of their day. After that, they were everything in the world—except teachers.

The system, for the teacher, was perfect. It was an open door to youthful opportunity. Teaching others, we taught ourselves. It was a marvelously maturing experience. At sixteen I was the teacher of farm boys older than myself. I had to be dignified, and, oh, so reserved, or I could never have gotten away with it. I was the object, in a community of grave Bohemian farmers, of the deference, as a supposed scholar, of wise men four times my foolish years.

To maintain the illusion of omniscience by which I was sustained, I had to work. Teaching, easier than farming or quarrying? It was the hardest work I have ever done. Six years of it and I was worn and weary, ready to seek some softer berth; for instance, as an editor.

Today teaching is, as it ought to be, of course, a learned profession. You learn before you teach, not by teaching as with me. The big school, in the day of big business, big government, is inevitable. Put a sixteen-year-old boy at the expert art of teaching school? A mule driver to piloting a plane? Yet one grave question stares at us: The intimacy in those little schools of teacher and taught by which Rachel Rymer and Harve Hamilton and Anna Ord made themselves warm memories and high examples when all they taught me is forgot—how can we have that influence and our big schools too?

12

Across the continent

In THE WEST VIRGINIA HILLS we went to bed by candle light, or, more likely, the light of the fireplace fire. The more venturesome were trying out that nineteenth-century novelty, prone to explode, the new oil lamp. Otherwise, we were of the eighteenth century.

We baked our corn bread in a covered spider buried in the fireplace coals. Our corn meal mush gained grace by long hours over that same fire in an iron pot hung from a hook. We made our own "soft soap." We traveled by ox-team, or, oftener, afoot. Every proper home had its spinning wheel. The women knitted, and many wove, incessantly.

Upon this seventeenth-century life of ours, the nineteenth, with the sign and symbol of its glory, the railroad and its trains, was swiftly rushing in. Then in a trice the twentieth, its motor cars, flying machines, rocket planes, relativity, atomic miracle! Six years before I was born, the Pacific railroad had reached its western goal. Earlier, the Baltimore and Ohio had slipped down West Virginia hollows from Washington to Cincinnati and the West, passing us seven miles away. But seven miles, in that time and land, was far. I saw my first railroad train when I was nine years old.

To us the railroad then and there was only an exciting novelty. Our seventeenth century did not need it. The sawlogs we marketed took the cheaper route. When the creeks were in flood we floated them down to the barges in the Ohio, a dozen miles away.

Now we were in Nebraska, a new world without water to float our goods. The railroad our seventeenth century had ignored was the very life of the nineteenth century into which now we had leaped. Of what use this fertile prairie soil if there be no way to carry its product to markets far away? Nebraska's corn, wheat, cattle, hogs had far to go. No town could thrive without its rail-road, its trains that stopped for freight and passengers. To be a railroad center was the kingly summit of a community's fortune and felicity.

The government, to encourage railroad building in the West, had subsidized the roads by gifts of land. Cities and counties voted bonds to lure the railways to their vicinity. This public money in some cases paid the whole cost of the private enterprise. The public paid for railroads which the builders were to own.

The railroad, so vital a source of life to us, became perforce a central interest, the dominant power over us. It supplied us jobs as section hands. I labored ten-hour days, one summer as a youth, cutting August weeds on the Burlington right of way. The local station agent was ex-officio an outstanding citizen. The section boss matched him for eminence. Pat Lyman, conductor and dictator of our passenger train, was a haughty man to whom we all paid deference. As to the most high men above, the division superintendent, the roadmaster, the very president of the line, this brings us to czars and emperors. For we were dependent on the railroads and they knew it and acted accordingly. The brakeman on the passenger train might, on occasion, condescend amiably, but fraternize, as with equals? Not he.

My first summer in Nebraska we lived in a two-room house beside the railroad track. That was a privilege I have never ceased to prize. I watched the comings and goings of the trains as a lover might watch and wait for his beloved. Each belching, coughing locomotive I knew by number as a friend. Jim Harrington, the station agent, I adored at a distance as only a boy can worship a high and handsome man. Meekly I dreamed. Suppose some day I should become such a station agent as Jim Harrington, with his mastery of the chattering telegraph! Some of my bolder and more brilliant boyhood mates were actually to attain that height. As for me, a yet more reckless dream awoke. It became my vaulting ambition to sit with my hand on the throttle and my eye on the track as nothing less than the mighty engineer himself.

There in the railroad we lived and moved and had our being—not the dreaming small boys only, but everyone. And as we looked up to the railroads, so they looked down on us. Since they were the source of our being, ought we not bow down and worship them? We could have supposed that a power so potent were better our servant than a master over us. That bold and revolutionary view came later. We had not thought of it then.

So as not to be troubled by meddlers, the railroad men came to operate our politics even as they ran their trains. A thoughtful distribution of free rides and such privileges as sites on sidetracks for grain elevators, lumber yards and industries, did much to keep our politics in hand. The Burlington named the senator from south of the Platte, the Union Pacific the north-of-the-Platte senator. As to governor, they might alternate.

The railroad, introducing the age of speed, was at the summit of its power and glory when I was mowing weeds on the right of way for a dollar and fifteen cents a day. But the times were changing. Power had made itself tiresome, as power always does. In 1890 a Populist Legislature appeared in Lincoln with plans for state regulation of railroad rates, the eight-hour day and other radical things. And rolling in stately instability down the road, scaring the farmers' horses, came the great nineties with the next era of speed, the unbelievable bicycle.

That row of moving heads, reared against the prairie sky, could it be a camel train? My book of travels in the Holy Land had pictures of the sort. But this was the land of the bison, of the belligerently lowered head, not of the haughty camel. As the procession, on that sunny summer morning in the year 1885, came near, I saw that the traveling heads were human, not animal.

The heads surmounted bodies, each perched, not on a horse or camel, but on a single high revolving wheel. The Lincoln Bicycle Club was abroad for a Sunday airing and a display of athletic agility. In single file they rode in stately dignity, each man astride his wheel.

How did he stay up there? A tail-like appendage curved back and down from the summit of the big wheel to a little wheel which followed, preserving a precarious balance for the rider perched above. By pedals at the hub of the big wheel the rider kept up his motion and preserved his poise.

As I stood astonished at the sight, the leader of the procession failed to note a small obstruction—a corncob or a clod—in the wheel-track ahead of him. The big wheel hit it and was checked. The momentum of the rider carried him ahead. In a twinkling the man atop the wheel was prone on the ground, his wheel on top of him. The man whose wheel had hit the clod crept from under his machine, laughed cheerfully, dusted off his clothes, remounted and was on his precarious way again.

Merely mounting these things was high adventure. You hopped along behind, one foot on a step in the frame, to get up speed. Then with a leap you rose into the saddle. If you leaped too far, over the handlebars you went. It was an activity for the young, bold and opulent. No rider of the pony express ever traded his pony for a high-wheeled bicycle. Then progress, as always, came. This plaything for the reckless became, by ever so simple a trick, the means for a brief but dizzy age of speed. The low-built safety bike, easy for everyone, was here to upset our world. With its awful speed of fifteen miles an hour or so it gave each man of us a railroad train of his own.

Were I to visit the capital, a dozen miles away, I could defy Pat Lyman, the dictator of the train. I could save my thirty-five cents fare. I could mount my bike, whenever I was ready, and go. Here was new liberty.

The solid tire gave way quickly to the cushion, then the pneumatic tire. The age of independent luxury had dawned. In the bicycle, in the nineties, we lived and moved and had our being. Our talk was of tires and gear ratios and the merits of wooden, as against metal frames and handlebars. When genius contrived the coaster brake our felicity was complete. Nature alone had done no better than give us plodding legs. But nature gave us brains, and brains had now produced these easy rolling wheels. Spurning the once indispensable railroad, I rode one hundred and ten miles one day.

The worries this new age of wild speed produced! The farmers' horses took on a vast hysteria. Pedestrians, attuned to slower times, fell foul of the flying "hot rodders" on their bikes. The social and political problems of the bicycle age of speed grew ominous. What were we coming to? Of a sudden, our bicycle problems at their peak, what was this coming, churning and chugging, down the road, crushing the chickens and frightening the children in its path? It was bold Dr. Finney in the first eruption of that impossible contraption, derided by all conservatives, the rushing, stalling, terror-spreading motor car!

The disconsolate bike! Who has mind for rabbits when the lion roars?

13

Omnipresent politics

OUT ON THE DUSTY NINE MILE PIKE, in front of my Grandfather Shields' two-room log house, I was shouting at the top of lusty five-year-old lungs: "Hurrah for Hancock!"

Pinned to my cotton waist was a red ribbon on which a printed rooster crowed. Beneath the rooster in black letters were the names: "Hancock and English." What the ribbon and all my hurrahing meant I had, of course, no least idea.

A political campaign was on and I was being indoctrinated, thus early, into a Democrat. Gen. Hancock, a soldier who knew no more of politics than to call the tariff a local issue, was the Democratic candidate for President. My father and grandfather were for him, and so, of course, was I. So come, by heredity, the shapes of our noses and our politics.

The Civil War was then but fifteen years past. That cataclysm had supplied the emotions which were to affect men's political attitudes for decades afterward. The war had planted the Republican party in apparent permanent control of the government. I learned early the wisdom of doing my Democratic cheering before the counting of the votes. The shooting had stopped in '65, but men were still voting "as they had shot" for most of the ensuing century.

In our hills the long dead Andrew Jackson was still a living power. My grandfathers, when I came upon the scene, were voting faithfully for Old Hickory. In those days voting made on our minds no onerous demands. We were born to politics as to our names.

Now I was off to the West where Democrats were a novelty and from all directions came new pressures on all minds. I came from the scanty economy of my independent, self-sufficient West Virginia Uncle John to the plenty, with its ill-working interdependence, which made scarcity for my Nebraska Uncle Jim.

What is it makes up our minds for us? My father was a thoughtful man. He weighed the issues gravely as they rose. The tariff, the money question, the railroad question received his careful scrutiny. Always, in the end, he approved the position taken by the Democrats. Always, in the end, our Republican neighbors approved the position taken by the Republicans.

Yet minds can change. In the West to which I came in 1884 the plight of the pioneer farmers was straining fiercely at these sacred party ties. It was forcing many of us to the desperate extremity of thinking for ourselves. Our neighbor state of Kansas had won in 1888 the glory of giving the largest of all majorities to Harrison, Republican candidate for President. Nebraska was hardly less one-sided at the polls.

Two years later Kansas was swept by the Populists. A senator without a necktie and a congressman without socks were sent to speak for Kansas in Washington. The long pent waters of revolt broke free. Republican Nebraska, at the same time, elected a Populist legislature and a Democratic governor!

I was to spend my life studying the movements of the minds of men, especially in the field of politics. We change the shape of our minds, I was to see, hardly more easily than the length of our legs. The mind is no feather in the wind. It is fiercely tough, as stubborn as a stone. But a stone, I had learned on my rockpile, is not impregnable. Attack it by sheer force, a violent master stroke, and you have a shattered hammer handle for your pains. Reason gently with the rock, chip it with subtle strokes, a bit on this side and a bit on that, and the boulder is dissolved.

I find myself suspicious of any trick or art for the quick changing and molding of the minds of men. Men's minds, like their motor cars, must take their curves slowly or be upset. I am relieved to remember that, though in professional folly I have often tried in a hurry to turn men's minds, no proof of my success was ever to be found. I view with alarm the new techniques and instruments with their threatening power to stampede voters en masse down steep places into seas.

The revolt of the farmers in my new world was no sudden whim. It was the flowering of a long-growing discontent, product of a long-felt need. I have noted through the decades what a glacial pace the minds of men together take; but there is never a total freezing of the mind. The movement is always there. The lack of it would be death.

Nor was the play of politics wholly a distant, party thing. Was ever politics anywhere more potent and pressing than school politics?

The old time school district, as I knew it as a pupil, then as a teacher, was a world in itself, our smallest unit of government. A board of three governed the school district—a director, a moderator, a treasurer. In annual meetings the people met to elect the trustees, vote a tax levy and express themselves as they might please on school affairs. In this miniature school-district democracy was all that play of human nature familiar to the larger field of the nation and of the states.

Our village maintained two churches, Methodist and Lutheran. In an unspoken way, two parties, these churches their core, appeared. The Methodists were more numerous and usually named the board. One year they were caught napping. A Lutheran farmer was elected school director. Here I had, at a very early age, my personal introduction to the spoils system in politics. That change in administration cost me my four-dollars-a-month job as schoolhouse janitor. The "spoils of office" went to a Lutheran boy.

The school board selected the teacher, but the people were not backward with their advice. They approved the teacher or he looked elsewhere for his next year's job. In that little republic of letters, a village school district, I was to have, thanks to a people's democratic assertiveness, a most sobering, salutary experience. My pride was to have a wholesome fall. I had taught for a second year my school of Bohemian farmers (an experience which made me a lifelong Czechophile). Then I moved up to a village school nearer home, with higher pay. Here, too, perhaps just to prove that I could, I stayed a second year.

I could have stayed on. They called me a good teacher. I wasn't. I was merely a successful sitter on a lid. How could one be a good teacher of seventy pupils ranging from five to twenty years of age? I had, for a fact, kept the school in control, a matter of primary consequence. Ready for wider worlds to conquer, I looked around. My home school had a principal to choose.

One rule for a youth setting out to teach was: Stay away from the home school. It will be a hornet's nest. They know too much about you there. Go away, where you can maintain a stranger's dignity. I had started thirty miles away. My next stop was seven miles away. Surely now I could defy the rule and venture the rest of the way. The fool would rush in where angels feared.

I had lived in the village since I was nine years old. Who lives in such a community lives in a goldfish bowl. Your private life is public property. If there were aught against me, the skies would have emblazoned it. So one might have thought. The board announced its decision—and the sky fell on its head and mine.

Miss Sally Forrest, prim and proper spinster, took to the sidewalks to save the school from me. Casper Dice, the blacksmith who had made to order the special hammer with which I had crushed the concrete before the concrete crusher crushed me, added his veto to hers. Two neighbor farmers whom I had humbly helped in harvest time joined in the campaign.

How many in all there were I did not know or ask. I remember, with such scant pride as the event permits, that I had the sense to hold my tongue. I went my way, adding nothing to the din. One thing I needed to know. What was wrong with me that this storm should have been raised? Miss Forrest, the grim, prim spinster, had made her grievance clear. We had met on the street and I had not spoken to her. The charge of the rest was, in general, that I was an upstart and "stuck up."

They were right. I saw it then and see it still. I was getting what was coming to me, a calling down for which I have been grateful ever since. I was not, in fact, "stuck up." The opposite was true. I had been the raggedest of the ragged, the poorest of the poor. Far from looking down on anyone, I expected to be looked down on by everyone. If I hadn't spoken to "Aunt Sally" Forrest it was because I was bashfully waiting for her to speak first to me. If this led to a reserve which looked like "uppishness," how were people to know the difference?

I had been too mindful of myself, not enough of other folk. A good lesson, a chastening experience, that beating brought to me. Before the time for the school term to start, an alluring post in a distant region was offered me. To the relief of my friends and the joy of the rest I withdrew from the battlefield at home.

14

Paradise lost

In my old geographies what is now on the map as Oklahoma was Indian Territory. Indian tribes cajoled and crowded from their eastern homes by relentless whites had been granted refuge here. These included the "five civilized tribes" of which the smallest was the Seminoles. Their twenty-five hundred people owned and occupied the center of the region, a modest county in extent.

When Spinster Sally Forrest, whom I had failed to speak to, banished me for my uppishness from my hometown teaching job, she hoisted me inadvertently into this land of the Seminoles. It was a land of pure delight. With money paid the Seminoles for yielding up their home in Florida, two academies, Mekusukey for boys, Emehaka for girls, were established in their new home. To Mekusukey, a three-story brick building set on a low hill and towering over a scattered wood, I came as the school's "disciplinarian." I was to keep order. That proved, in this "savage" community, a simple task.

Here was a world I had dreamed of but had never hoped to see. In the West Virginia hills I had lived the life of the eighteenth century. Here, among these aboriginal Americans, I was to live in the time of Homer or, who knows, the time of Moses, or Methuselah.

It was a lovely land, level enough for comfort and hilly enough to ease the eye. It was forest and prairie, both in one. Everywhere, save in the few small clearings, there were trees; but the trees were so scattered as to give the grass a share of sun. No fences obstructed the way. A few trails, mere wheel tracks, there were; but when you chose your direction you set off straight, needing no highway, making your own path.

The Seminoles were getting their living from this land without defacing it. They merged into the scene, no more disturbing

it than the deer in the thickets or the fish in the streams. They
built their little homes in nooks invisible from the trails. We
could ride the fourteen miles from Mekusukey to Wewoka, the
capital, and never see a house. Yet homes were hidden all around.
These people we called savages occupied their land without
despoiling it. We could never say of them, as we say in shame
of ourselves in viewing a scene once pure and undefiled: "Men
have been here. See the little they have left, the ruin they have
wrought."

In this new world my education in politics and government
proceeded rapidly. The Seminoles had their own sovereignty,
their own politics. But here were no parties, no spoils of office,
no conflicts, as far as I could see, of rival ambitions or interests.

The tribe was made up of fourteen bands or clans. These
bands, not any territorial space, were the roots of the government.
Each band chose from its number two members of the legislature,
the council. The council made the laws and chose a governor.

This was the government, a perfect simplicity, a practical
democracy. The only paid officers of the government were the
national police, a handful of mounted men.

Left to themselves, the Indians might even have dispensed
with these. There was no serious tension or turbulence among
themselves. Only to cope with the white man who invaded their
land with his liquor was this force required. The civilized white
man was the one serious menace to the peace of these savage
Indians.

This government worked with a smoothness and efficiency
not expected of any government. So simple and so close to the
people it was, there was little room for evils to creep in. No sign
of abuse or corruption did I ever see. Nor was there any mark
of discontent among the people with their condition or with their
government. Theirs was a free economy, the one really free economy I have ever seen. Each man worked as pleased him, needing
no other man's control. If some were more prosperous, others
less, that merely reflected the difference in their skill and energy.
Here all men were really born equal—equal in opportunity.

How far this freedom grew from one peculiar trait of the
Seminole economy I do not now discuss. That peculiar way was

this: The Seminole owned for himself whatever he made the land produce. The land itself he could not own. That, like the air and the sun, was a common heritage. The nation owned the land. The citizen could occupy such land as he would put to productive use, that and no more. Each Seminole child had at its birth its free and equal access to the soil. It needed pay no man for a foothold on the earth on which, by no consent of its own, it had been cast.

For his simple economy the Indian needed no vast fields. There was land enough for all. Since every man was free to make, on the soil, his own job, there could be no involuntary unemployment, no unwilling poverty. What was this but the Utopia of which, through the ages, men have dreamed?

What would have come of the world of these Seminoles, quiet, secure and content in their Utopia, had they been let alone? Living neither rich nor poor but free, they were as secure in their paradise as Adam and Eve seemed in theirs. A little patch of corn, a little wood gathered for a fire, a saunter in the woods for game, and the Seminole's work was done. Now he could sit in the sun and vegetate, like a happy turtle on his log, or he could sit in the sun and meditate, a saint or a Socrates. He was free to stand or run. He could mount the skies on a wishful wind or stay contented on the ground.

Amid our hurrying and our worrying we dream of that region of hills and vales in ancient Greece which we know as Arcadia. The hunters and shepherds dwelling there, piping their pleasure in the sun or shade, lived peaceful, playful lives which have been the envy of men ever afterwards. Here now, before my eyes, in my own America, lay ancient Arcadia.

The boys at Mekusukey stumbled, in school hours, through the alphabet. They came to count a little and to add and multiply. They learned a little of our language which, once home again, they soon forgot. The rest of the day, out of doors, or, when the weather was cold, in the Academy furnace room, they returned to their hearts' desire. Here was the education they were never to forget. They took skins of squirrels and made them into bowstring. They took sinews of rabbits to fasten to their arrows the heads of flint they chipped. They shaved lengths of wood into supple bows and aimed for the eye of the peering possum or the skulking wolf.

They had no quarrel, these simple folk, over what a child should know. They consented with faith to the books the white men brought. But first of all, the boy must learn to be master of his world. He must be swift and skilled to serve his needs in prairie, wood and stream. Here was a people whose problems had been solved. Each man was maker of his own destiny. Since there could be no unwilling idleness, there could be no problem of poverty. Each citizen was free, by his own self-chosen labor, to serve or neglect his own necessities. If he was hungry, he deserved no help or sympathy.

What would its future have been had this Indian Eden been allowed to live? We were not allowed to know. This cool wild flower of the prairie woods, this Indian democracy, was too simply good to survive the white man's greed. It obstructed the white man's way. He wanted this Eden for his own, for progress, as he said. He appealed to Washington. The Indian way was not our way. The Indian must be Americanized.

So this Indian nation, by act of Congress, was destroyed. There must be "free enterprise." The land was "allotted" as private property to the individual Indians. The white men then, in the old routine of beads and bottles, lured their land away from them. Forty years afterward I viewed the tumbling ruin which had been Mekusukey Academy. I asked for Billy Bowlegs and Wiley Harjo and Chili Ross and all the boys I had long before seen on their way to the secure, serene life which was the prospect then of every Seminole.

Such as survived were hired laborers or living on relief. The Indian Eden of forty years before was becoming a smoking, disheveled, roaring white man's prosperity. Gone is Arcadia. "The Great Pan is dead." I was standing at the ruins of a murdered Utopia. I now possess, as memento and symbol of a lost paradise, filched from crumbling Mekusukey—a broken brick.

15

World of a book or two

THERE WAS A GATHERING in my home on Painter Creek. What it was about, I was too young then to understand. That there was much quoting of the Scriptures, even at the age of eight I could recognize. Jake Tifner was saying: "Blessed are the peacemakers." Some one was admonishing some one else: "Bear ye one another's burdens." My Aunt Charlotte was remembering that "a soft answer turneth away wrath." My old grandfather, himself a fighting Irishman, was exhorting the assembly: "If it be possible, as much as lieth in you, live peaceably with all men."

The meeting broke up in the end with hand-shaking all around as if some great good had been achieved. Indeed it had been, as I was afterward to know. Pat Peters and his wife had quarreled and were about to part. That, in the hills, was a supreme tragedy. This gathering in my father's house was a peace conference. The contending pair had been prevailed upon to come. The elders of the church were there with Scripture on their tongues. The duty of wives to submit to their husbands; the equal duty of husbands to love their wives; it was a great day for St. Paul. In the end the quarreling couple promised to make up and keep the peace. Good Mrs. Wilson urged them:

> *If at first you don't succeed,*
> *Try, try again.*

This, it happened, was not from the Bible but from our other much quoted authority, McGuffey of the reading books.

These two books, in the West Virginia hills, encompassed us round about. The Bible was the textbook of the church. Its place and power the peace conference there on Painter Creek revealed. McGuffey, his *Readers*, were the textbooks of the school. From the spider and the fly to "try, try again" we found our wisdom there.

I was to find that a book, the while we are buried in it, is our world. It is our life, our self. In it we live and move and have our being. We need be careful as to the book to which we so commit ourself. The command it takes over us as we read will be obeyed long after the reading has been done. I was always to be in the grasp of these two books.

The fare McGuffey chose for us depicted a plain piety, a stern morality. Life was real, life was earnest. The grave was not its goal. The path of righteousness to which he consigned us was narrow, rough, and steep. Crime brought its punishment here, to say nothing of hereafter. But virtue had a visible reward. I have had occasion, under the impact of events, to hold some reservations as to these exterior rewards.

In McGuffey, the good were paid for their goodness. The widow who gave her last herring to the stranger at her door was to find that stranger her long lost son, returned to support her in luxury. But when I nobly confessed to my mother that it was I who raided the sugar bowl, she switched me sharply, a common discipline in those rude days. Disillusioned, I saw that the cash value of virtue could not be counted on. If it could be, indeed, it would not be virtue, but merely business sense. A world that bribes its children with candy to be good goes back to the good McGuffey, in like way trying to lure us heavenward.

Our other book took the higher, harder ground. There, too, faith and courage were to triumph, but when nailed upon a cross. We must lose our life to save it. Such was the hard saying with which our world has been wrestling feebly two thousand years.

That library of history, fiction, parable, politics, morals and supernal vision, the Bible, has been, through all my years, the subject of unending argument. Some have worshiped it "from kiver to kiver," as the people at our Painter Creek peace conference did, as the divinely dictated total of all truth. Others, like Robert G. Ingersoll, have scoffed at it. Evolution, the skeptic has said, disproved it. It has been undermined by the omnipresent hypocrite. Its defenders have disputed its meaning among themselves. There were as many versions of the Scripture as of the blind men's elephant. Did not even the devil, as Shakespeare said, cite Scripture to serve his purposes?

It was my happiness, soon, to be done with the arguing. The poet Cowper, a devout man, gave the clue. He prayed the gods who rule the tongue, supposing, as St. James denies, that such there are, to deliver him from a "duel in the form of a debate." Whenever was bad made wiser, better, by that rage of contending egos which goes as argument? I had the help, too, of my McGuffey, his tale of the traveler with the sun and wind disputing as to which could make him doff his cloak. The wind blew. The traveler held his cloak the closer. The sun shone warm. Off came the cloak. The violence of argument had lost. Peaceful persuasion had prevailed.

Fleeing the battles about the Bible, I turned to the Book itself. Years afterward Dr. David Fairchild, the noted botanist, told me a story which would have served me then. A gathering of botanists in his home on Biscayne Bay was disputing the character of a certain tree. The argument grew heated. Tempers were becoming frayed. At last Dr. Fairchild remarked: "There's a tree of the kind in the yard. Let's stop our talk about it and go look at it."

Stopping this arguing I found myself wandering with Moses in the wilderness. I am still wandering in the wilderness, for that is life. In the wandering of Moses and the wandering centuries since all history is revealed. What wanderers in the wilderness, stumbling, blind, sometimes following a star, sometimes a will-o'-the-wisp, have all nations, all peoples, all men and women been!

Each seeks the place of his dreams, some promised land of peace and rest—a home. One falls by the wayside and another struggles on. Some reach the promised land they sought and then, through want of sustaining wisdom, forfeit it! Many a Moses have men followed as the centuries crept by. We call George Washington one. How his people murmured against him when the bitter waters of Marah touched their tongues! Ben Franklin, at the court of King James, was a Moses demanding: Let my people go. Many a Pharaoh, in my own times, has been called upon to let a people go.

We go on to the sequel of the story and see what sorry use, once their seas have parted and they are free, men often made of their liberty. I lost my first pocket knife, a ten-cent Barlow, the evening of the day my father brought it from town to me. As a four-year-old boy with his Barlow, so men with their liberty.

America the free, the beautiful, was a "promised land" to me. Would the promise be kept? In the Book I read clear and plain how a promised land, once gained, can be frittered away and lost. I read that "Jehoabaz . . . reigned seventeen years. And he did that which was evil in the sight of the Lord." Then came the consequence, the catastrophe. For in this book, unlike other stories you have ever read, the masters are not the rulers, but the ruled.

Above the kings and the peoples, unseen behind the world they see, a King of Kings prevails. "The Lord spake unto Moses." Where that voice was heard and heeded, there was health and strength. The promised land was safe. When that voice was slighted and grosser gods proclaimed, then woe! The spoiling of the temple! The captivity!

The hero of this book is not the man of power, the proud king. He is a Nathan standing stern, accusing, before the king, in a higher name warning him: You are the villain; thou art the man! In this book, as nowhere else, kings are not the judges but the judged. Here we ponder and perceive, not the ways of kings with men, but the way with kings of the "King of Kings."

Some, searching the Scriptures, proclaimed as history what others saw as poetry. Some saw as science what others, in Pilgrim's Progress way, perceived as parable. We disputed. To what use? As my world unfolded with the years, the great Book, absorbed with open mind, unfolded with it understandably. The poetry of Genesis and the science of Darwin, lamb and lion, lay down together. The fall of Adam and the rise of man, whether history or fable, was the story of mankind.

We argued evolution in the nineties as something new and strange. Here in the ancient Book itself was evolution—the onward striving in the wilderness of the mind and soul of man. He searched for God and his God grew as his own vision grew. The stern God of Sinai, the unfathomable God of Job, grew into the just God of Amos, the loving God of Isaiah, the universal God of Jesus with the simple rule:

What doth the Lord require of thee
But to do justly, and to love mercy,
And to walk humbly . . .

Here was the history of a seething world and of men wandering, yearning in the wilderness. Always the struggle! Jacob wrestled with the angel for his soul. Unwilling Moses, goaded by the bush, wrestled for his tribe. When men ceased to struggle they decayed. Some "flood" overwhelmed them and they died.

Was it water or the weight of their own evil ways destroyed the men of the Noah tale? How was it with Rome and Babylon and Assyria and Hitler? Here in the Book, as in the pages of history, the Sodoms, by one fire or another, are consumed. A people on the plain of Shinar planned their own proud self-serving way, forgetting a higher authority. Up went their tower, monument to their vanity. How many towers of Babel have tumbled since that one fell! A Babel of our own crashed in '29! Now we invade the atom where God was supposed to hide. Are we walking humbly? Another tower here? So goes the age-long story of men's pride and in their pride their fall. Through it all the seer, the prophet, seeing deep, lays down the final law: "Not by might, nor by power, but by my spirit, saith the Lord of hosts."

There was Genesis for overture. Then on with the wandering, its music, its murmuring, its battles, its bitter waters, its promised lands—lands to be won and lost, perhaps, again. Then at last the pause, the largo, where weary wandering men are comforted. "Come unto me, all ye that labor and are heavy laden, and I will give you rest." At last the happy ending, the mystic strains of Revelation, the vision of triumph at the end. "And there shall be no night there." The underlying, emerging law and wisdom to which our life is bound; the clue to history; the highway of the soul—all in a single cover, bound into a book. Its words confer a language with which, if we command it, we may say a volume in a phrase. Are we to be swine before which these pearls are cast?

16

Up, on and off

SCHOOL WAS OUT and Teacher Tom Davidson, saying goodbye, inquired of my lifetime plans. Was I going to be, he said, "a hewer of wood and a drawer of water?" At fifteen years I was not making plans at all. I mumbled something about getting a job in the quarry or on the farm. His question remained to simmer in my brain.

The fact was that once long before I had considered my future and had made a plan. That had been an experience too painful to repeat. The cousins left behind in the hills must have letters boasting of my new world in the West. On my knees before a kitchen chair for desk I penciled rosy, full accounts of the new life in the West. How cold or hot the weather, how everybody was, what everybody did—all this I reported voluminously.

I found I liked to write. It gave a clear field to talk about myself. In school, with Swinton's *Grammar*, I admired the way words fitted into sentences. The parts of speech became familiar friends. I could tell the difference between compound and simple and complex sentences. Roy Keys, my closest friend, could outrun me, outbet me, outwrestle me. But in juggling words in the grammar class he was no match for me. In the logical way of a free world, Roy became a wrestler with cattle on the farther plains. I was to wrestle, all my life, with words.

So writing letters, playing with words, I saw one day my future clear. I had been reading what other people wrote. How fine to write what other people read! I would be a writer. I would be just that. Fired with the new flame, I rushed home from school, burning to begin. I found a pencil and sharpened it. From my mother I begged a sheet of paper. Then at the kitchen table I sat down to write.

I sat down to write. An awful pause ensued. Then crashing upon me fell a catastrophic fact. There I was, all set to write;

and not a thing to say! How desolately often was that plight to recur in the writing years to come!

It was fun to be a boy. I say this, not forgetting that for me it has been more fun to be a man. Boys take a knocking around such as most grown men escape. But boys are resilient and their wounds are quickly healed. If they are poor they don't know it. If they are unhappy they get over it. There comes a time at last when the inevitable must be faced. A boy and his boyhood at last must part. He must be up and off.

Whether we like it or not, the years are inexorable. The boy must say with the apostle finally: "When I was a child . . . I understood as a child . . . But when I became a man, I put away childish things." The boy must put away childish things. He must be a man. Parting from my boyhood, I was to see as my life went on how I had parted with the greater half of me. As I take the backward look I see the most and best of me looming from afar. The first years have the making of the rest. Here grow the roots from which the fruits must come.

My world, at the parting time, was free, albeit poor. Youth, leaving boyhood, needs room for trying things, time to look around. My world was generous of that privilege. I had my August cutting weeds on the railroad right of way. The quarry rockpile was a boyhood school. I had a later turn with wheelbarrow, pick and shovel as a quarryman. The turns at farming almost captured me. I have always been ready, if my chosen work failed me, to turn without repining to the farm.

At sixteen came the chance to teach. Teaching in that day was a steppingstone—matrimony for the women, a business or profession for the men. As a starter I could find a school to teach. Young men parting from boyhood in that day could shop around. They might fail here only to do well there. So each might find, in due time, the niche that fitted him. The mates of my boyhood, by the time, as men, they had found themselves, were scattered from New England to Alaska. They were on farms, in mines, in schools, in stores, in offices—everywhere.

Two worlds, up to this time, I had had the happiness to explore. For a decade I had lived, in the hills and woods, the life of a vanished age. Years followed of village life on the youthful western plains. Now, boyhood left behind, yet another world beckoned me. Nebraska, which had become a state only in 1867, established two years later at Lincoln its university. Two Roca boys, both to become noted professors in universities, had already graduated there. Others from the village or nearby farms had become students there. Thither the ambition of all good spellers and the quick at arithmetic led. A preparatory course at the university served as high school for country youth. Now for the glory that was Greece, the greatness that was Rome, the new world of the mind! I was off to the university.

At the Battery in New York City I watched a ship discharge its cargo of immigrants. They spurted forth from the steerage, strange-appearing folk, their packs upon their backs, exploding anxiously, hopefully, into their new world. They reminded me of that September day when, a village youth, I was seeking entrance to the world of learning, to Nebraska University.

In the hills I had never seen a college, a college student, or a college graduate. The new home in the West was only a dozen miles, as distance goes in space, from the university. In hope, the distance was infinite. A year at the university, with the tuition only nominal, cost two hundred dollars at the least. Who, having two hundred dollars, could afford to spend it in that way? The higher education habit, even in the West, was then in its infancy. The free public school had but lately won its way. My mother had learned to read in a "subscription school." As to college for such as I, we never dreamed of it.

The tide, in the nineties, was rising. The inch of the country school was beginning to swell to the university ell. A few from the village community had gone forth, before I came, into the world of scholarship. A schoolmate, Robert Haile, whose speed of brain I could never match, saved enough from a year's teaching for a year as a "prep" at the university. Louis Deis, the blacksmith's son, swept a Lincoln lawyer's office for a place to sleep, worked as a waiter for his board. So sustained, he courted a scholar's life.

I had my two hundred dollars, saved from a teacher's salary, but would they let me in, a "prep"? From St. Peter at heaven's gate I had been taught to expect a kindly leniency. The stern

guardians of the academic heaven, what of them? Here was no
easy entering by way of a high school key. I must enter the
examination door. On my own I must get by with Cæsar, Euclid,
Myers' ancient history. I had tasted these limpingly at night,
studying alone. Now for the test.

Professor Fred M. Fling was hidden behind a newspaper
when I trembled into his office for the ordeal in history. He
lowered his paper after awhile and took a stern look at me. Did
I know where western civilization arose? I offered my guess.
How, he asked, did I know? An old hand at tracking rabbits,
I ventured again. By the footprints of language, I hazarded. "All
right; that's all. You'll do," he said, returning to his news.

That trial and acquittal took forty seconds by the clock. He
was a gruff man, Fred M. Fling. For that reprieve, had he been
Satan, I would love him still. I stumbled through the Latin test,
a babe in the classic woods. The young instructor, Josephine
Tremain, on whom my fate had hung, singled me out next day
in a roomful of country youth and whispered in my ear: "You
pass; seventy." Blessed damozel! She had given me, I suspected
then and am sure today, that passing grade for effort only. What
else could it have been?

Geometry! My mind, at sight of anything mathematical, has
always rolled over and acted dead. I turned in my paper, sure
that I had failed. The last proposition question I had muffed
utterly. I crept to my room, three city blocks away, disconsolate.
Arrived there, the answer to that last question flashed into my
mind. I rushed back to the classroom. The instructor was still
there. Would he let me answer that last question now? Heaven
forgive me for forgetting that saint's name! He smiled gently.
"No need," he said. "I've just looked over your paper. You've
passed." I was in!

We had straggled in, these boys and girls, not as a matter of
course, but as a matter of force, of personal hope and energy. Half
were sweeping offices and waiting table for their bed and board.
I had learned, living in an office and "batching it" for board,
how well one could live on a dollar or two a week. We had
come with a weird diversity of preparedness for our search. By
no smooth road and for no light purpose had we come. Were

the professor of history, the learned in Latin, the wizard of mathematics there to roll boulders in our path? If, with their tests, they looked us in the eye, rather than in our brains, were they the less wise for that?

I had tasted the sea-level democracy of the prairie, of the hills. Here was the gentler democracy of the academic heights. The learned professors on the peaks of knowledge, masters of their worlds, rolled about on their bicycles or walked, attentive to the awkward youth from the prairie villages. Here was the atmosphere of willing work. These youths had come at too much trouble to themselves to play away their time.

A happy new world with all around and above me friendly, helping on! A humbling, deflating world! Did I think, because I had spelled down the school at home that I was smart? Here were Alvin Johnson and Francis Philbrick and dozens more whose brains were at the goal before I was fairly on the way. Good for the bubble ego, that!

From the age of twelve I had never made it through a whole year at school. A breakdown of the eyes I had abused with too much reading always intervened. This heavenly year was to be no different. It was eye ache with its nerve strain, all the way. In April came the crash. The world of learning was not to be my home.

17

University afoot

WHEN AGING EYES, in the world of my youth, grew dim, they betook them to the store for a pair of spectacles. They picked over the stock displayed there, trying this pair and that, till the printed page came fairly clear. They paid the price, commonly a quarter of a dollar, and there they were.

That was only for old folks, Dr. Demaree said, when at last I took my aching eyes to him. I would have to see a city specialist. It would cost, he said, noting my alarm, only three or four dollars. I arrived at Dr. Dayton's office with a fortune, five dollars, got from somewhere by my ever resourceful mother. His fee and the new spectacles, he said, when all was done, would be seven and a half. The doctor was reasonable and generous. We compromised on the five I had.

I was twelve miles from home and penniless. It was past noon. I had no money for lunch. There was a train, Pat Lyman's local, but I had no thirty-six cents, the fare. There was but one thing to do. Under the yellow sun of an October day I walked and trotted that twelve miles. I reached home hungrier than ever I had been before or was ever to be afterward.

In the hills we had depended much upon our legs. With lack of roads and means to ride, our getting about was mostly done afoot. I remember a day when my mother walked seven miles to the family doctor with an aching tooth and seven miles home again. The hills and hollows around us were familiar to my feet.

On the prairies no one walked. Horses, self-supporting on the open range, were plentiful. Everybody rode. A man afoot, to browsing cattle an unfamiliar sight, might be attacked by them. Walking, in this world, had small place. I had forgotten I could walk. In this emergency I had to learn anew.

On the prairies with the cowboys, half horse, half man, we were in the van of the walkless age now upon us in full swing.

The farmers were even beginning to ride as gentlemen when they plowed their fields.

Now, spurred by bitter necessity, I had walked that twelve miles and no harm had come of it. I must even have enjoyed it, else how the bright memory I hold of that October trot?

Those errant eyes of mine were to be, through all my life, a thorn in the flesh, a stumbling block. Yet to them I was to owe the discovery of a world, the world afoot, a world of free delight. These rebellious eyes had bestowed upon me this twelve-mile tramp. "Afoot and lighthearted," from that time forth, I would "take to the open road."

The next year after that compulsory twelve-mile tramp I was teaching a country school with a boarding place four miles away. Two years of that, then a school to teach seven miles from home, reached by train in the morning, back afoot at night.

What went on inside the schoolroom those four years has grown dim in my memory. Those walks with their clouds and sunshine, cold and heat, and a mind free to roam, remain a clear and radiant memory. Is there something of worship in walking that it should so keenly record itself? What of the walking on the shores of Galilee, and that strange story of the walk to Emmaus? Walking and thinking, are they not cause and effect, effect and cause? What of Aristotle and his "walking-about" teaching, the "peripatetic" philosophy? Here is Ralph Waldo Emerson saying how a walk abroad, a "quest for river grapes," healed his worst wounds.

I had delighted intemperately in books. With eyes buried in a book, the book was my world. I was blind to the world of which the book could be but a reflection, nothing more. The eyes rebelled. Debarred from books, what could I do? I could walk. Better, of course, both text and tramp, each in its right degree. But when losing the one leads to finding the other, the mourner can be comforted.

Legs, a biologically-minded neighbor of mine predicts, will yet become obsolete and disappear. Our work, even the soldier's and the farmer's, is now done sitting down. Escalators supplant the stairs. Should one want to walk, where can he walk? The world is made for riders. The walkers, if they would not be crushed, must stand aside. Our legs, shriveled by disuse, are they to be as the vermiform appendix, as the ostrich's wings? Was ever an inspiration got at sixty miles an hour?

Would I lose that red letter September day when I rose with morning star and walked thirty miles to see a friend, arriving in time for lunch? And the time, with a companion rich in mind, on a walking week in the Ozarks, happily bewaring the ravening wood ticks every April hour? Those miles of literary lore with sharp George Woods to set the mental pace—my introduction to Dostoevski and "Crime and Punishment," the dead Russia of yesterday? Such the unforgettable hours when aching eyes sent me forth to turn to gold on the open road the leaden hours barred from books!

The books I have read I have more or less forgot. These walks and talks on the open road, under the open sky, my world afoot, remain, with the friendships they sealed, a healing memory.

The profit in walking is a matter of taking both head and eyes along. My early mentor here was Dan Haskin, one of the older Roca boys. Dan was no prodigy with books. My head hardly reached his elbow, yet he and I read together in school of the boy with open eyes and the boy with as good as none. But in the world outside no one could keep up with Dan. The fields, the woods and the waters were home, his world, to him. They were his vocation, his happiness.

The leaves were unfolding and the flowers blooming and Teacher Tom Davidson taught us to note the shapes of leaves. They were cordate, peltate, ovate, lanceolate, linear and the rest. We were to describe their various margins: serrate, crenate, entire and the rest. Leaves were simple and compound and their veins were palmate or otherwise.

We were to gather leaves and arrange them with respect to these characters; and of course each plant must have a name. There was to be a prize for the largest collection of properly described leaves. With an eye on Dan Haskins, I joined the race.

Dan was too much a child of nature to hurry in a race. Would he strain a point to help a friend? I raise, not answering, a doubt. When I came upon a milkweed leaf prodigious in size, Dan said gravely, "That is the mammoth milkweed."

Whether Asa Gray ever heard of that special species I carefully never have inquired. Neither, I surmise, did the judge of the contest, Tom Davidson. I came up with five hundred and twenty-three leaves, real, or alleged by Dan. The closest contender, lacking the help of Dan, had four hundred and eighty-nine.

No scientist would concede my communion with Dan the dignity of botany. What of that? When aching eyes, years later, spewed me out of doors afoot, there on the ground or rustling a welcome in the wind were the leaves my boyhood labors knew. It was only print, not leaves on trees, that seared my eyes. Out of doors, with the flowers and weeds, and the trees the plainsmen were quick to plant, I found myself at home as with old friends.

There were yet more friends to be, with whom I had not been as lucky as with leaves. The leaves were in the reception line outdoors. I could call them by their names—at least the names Dan Haskins gave to them. But what of the stars, the birds, the clouds, calling unseeing eyes? My earlier education had failed me there. More was to come.

Do I seem extreme in appraising the wealth that walking has brought to me? Then I must out with it. The stars bring me to it. I walked into a wife. We went walking, she and I; not just a pitiful around a block or two, but out on the hills where the sky was clear and the stars were close. It was August, a rich month, as any viewer afoot should know, for stars.

Overhead was Corona, the kingly crown. In the south were Scorpio and the milk dipper. Lyra, with Vega transcendant, was high in the sky, with Aquila not far away. The Big Dipper did its pointing and the Little Dipper was in its place; Leo, the sickle, was sinking in the west. Arcturus was at its best. Altair in the eagle was bright and Perseus was scraping the horizon in the north. Cassiopeia of the broken-backed chair was courting Polaris as was her wont.

How do I, a fugitive from the schools, know all this? Because we went walking, she and I. The stars were there and she saw them though I was blind to them. And if she insisted on keeping my head in the heavens while we walked, and if she taught me those higher things, the stars, have I then no right to boast?

We went walking and called the stars by name and lived happy
ever afterward.

Out in the world, walking, I found my old friends, my half
a thousand leaves. I knew the green world by its leafy countenance. I was to know the stars. I was total stranger to the birds.

Ah, our no-eyes race:

> *The heavens call you, and around you burn,*
> *And yet ye walk, eyes fastened on the ground.*

I was acquainted slightly, when cast forth on the unknown
outdoor world, with the loquacious crow. (If we slit his tongue,
he could talk.) The mating moan of the prairie chicken I could
not help but hear. The robin, because it was harbinger of spring,
even I knew. But what of the hundreds of kinds of birds that
came our way as the year went 'round? They had flashed by
me unseen.

Here was life itself, its ebb and flow expressed in the flight
of the myriad birds, of all the year the brightest moving show.
There are men accounted wise who rejoice in a new bird found
even as Croesus at each new million amassed. Nor could we call
the latter the richer, happier. So in the end, among the leaves,
stars, birds and highways, my bookless education had its hope.

18

The Fortieth Street Road

Southward from the city for a dozen miles straight over rolling lands runs an extension of Lincoln's Fortieth Street. It skirts the stone quarries and ends where my boyhood village begins. Other roads to the city, more level and smooth, were preferred by travelers awheel. The Fortieth Street Road from my city lodging to my heart's home in the country was left to me, afoot.

Mile on mile I could plod with never a rival to share the solitude. I trod my road in spring when the fields were plowed brown and the white-painted farmsteads, with their clumps of painfully planted, protecting trees, stood cameo-like against the land. I loped down its distances with howling blizzards at my back, making more miles per hour than was counted right for a pedestrian. I knew that road in its every aspect, its every mood. The Fortieth Street Road and I were never-failing friends.

One thing a compulsory pedestrian learns to his vast gain. For walking, all weather is good. Rain, shine, cold, hot, calm, blustery—each bears its special gift, confers its peculiar joy. Who waits on the weather for a walk will never learn what walking ought to be.

Every fence held in summer its meadowlark with the swinging, ringing whistle of the free-speaking bird. I tried to put into human speech the various comments of this versatile vocalist. It clearly inquired: "What do the pee-pul do?" In more hurried tempo it commented on the scene afield. "Bran new cultivator," chuckling, it would say. My last sight of the vanishing prairie hen in that region came on the Fortieth Street Road. A howling wind from the northwest swept the bird from up Wyoming way with fixed, spread wing before it. On that one road there were never two walks the same. Of each and every journey there is a story, a memory of its own.

Here it was, then, I stumbled, thanks to the weary eyes that
drove me forth, upon another world, a new world that has softened my old envy of Christopher Columbus and all other dis-
coverers. I went forth for a walk and found another world, the
world of poetry.

All days were good on the Fortieth Street Road; yet I confess
a special tenderness for October there. At the thought of October's
yellow days on the Fortieth Street Road, a rush of poets' frenzies
fills my mind. The first to flash before me is apt to be the lines,
first quoted by a fellow traveler on this very road:

> *A haze on the far horizon,*
> *The infinite, tender sky,*
> *The rich ripe tints of the cornfields . . .*

and the rest, with its: "Some of us call it Autumn, and others call
it God."

It was such an October day on the Fortieth Street Road that
brought the new planet, poetry, swimming into my sky. From
childhood I had dreamed my days away. I would start a story,
commonly with myself as center, in the "to be continued" style.
From day to day I would elaborate on that dream. I rose, on the
wings of one such early dream, from station agent to president
of the road. Thus I could while a walk away.

Why should the mind grind on such emptiness? Why not
give it substance to gnaw upon? I could swallow enough food in
half an hour to keep digestion going half a day. To be nourished
in body there was no need to be eating all the time. To be
nourished in mind I did not need to be reading all the time.
Read deep awhile; then, resting the eyes, take time to digest it
well.

At school in the city I lodged in the office of Don L. Love,
a lawyer and a philosopher, paying for the privilege with mop
and broom. I put the problem to him. In what form can one get
the most food for the mind with the least strain of the eye? He
answered: Poetry. Great poetry, he said, is the sap of life and sum
of knowledge boiled down to the syrup of wisdom, intelligence.
Poetry as rhyme and story I had long enjoyed. The poem as life
and wisdom, that was yet to come.

One morning on the Fortieth Street Road I had watched a sunrise with a feeling of baffled futility. My eyes told me it was exquisite. I found I could not feel what my eyes declared. I was alien to the glory there. And often, on the road, I had been aware of more around me than my eyes could see or feelings grasp. I was not equal to my opportunity. The world and sky spoke a language I did not understand. I was hungry, needing to be fed. As Don Love had said, I should try the poets.

On that particular day I had carried with me on the Fortieth Street Road a slip of paper, the song of a poet I did not know:

> *And I, too, sing the song of all creation,*
> *A brave sky, and a glad wind blowing by,*
> *A clear trail and an hour for meditation,*
> *A long day and the joy to make it fly,*
> *A hard task, and the muscle to achieve it,*
> *A fierce noon and a well-contented gloam,*
> *A good strife and no great regret to leave it,*
> *A still night and the far red lights of home.*

In a mile I had it in memory. In that mile the Fortieth Street Road was lighted and lengthened into a world to travel through, a way to carry on. Such is the way of the poet. His words are a yeast to ferment and swell in the mind containing them, into more than a book, into more than a shelf of books—into a life.

Here was a crack in the doorway to a world where one word of gold, without the least strain of eye, can work the magic of volumes of weary words of clay. So came my secret joy and shame—an alliance with the poets the world was passing by.

On Friday afternoons in the days of Rachel Rymer and Tom Davidson we laid by our spelling books for a speaking bee. Every pupil had his "piece." Bravely we labored with Mary's little lamb and the boy on the burning deck. Eloquent Frank Dunham stirred us with "Spartacus to the Gladiators." His sister, Anna, was supreme in "Curfew Shall Not Ring Tonight."

My highest flight as a boy orator was attained with John Townsend Trowbridge's prophetic epic, "Darius Green and His Flying Machine." Darius Green was the Yankee lad who said, reasonably enough: "The birds can fly, and why can't I?" Then, true boy that he was, he set out, with ensuing bruises as the poem at length portrayed, to fly.

Half a century later I was to live in Dayton, a neighbor and friend of Orville Wright, the Darius Green who was really at last to fly; for some man finally does what others determinedly dream. I never saw that gentle, modest immortal Orville Wright but my tongue reverted to the lines stored in memory in those far show-off days.

The winter literary and debating society, a community boon in those unexciting days, gave further scope to oratorical aims. Poetry, since in that day it rhymed, served better to recite than prose. I was early fluent in such masterpieces as Byron's Battle of Waterloo, with its "sound of revelry by night"; the Ride of Paul Revere; the sad May Queen of Tennyson. Thanks to this early speaking "in public on the stage" the memorizing of verse was nothing new to me. The poetry of the platform was drama, making a story shine. Poetry as a makeshift education, a mental concentrate, a rest for eyes, as my friend Don Love proposed it, was deeper, different. To take to the poets was to go against the tide. The age of speed was just then getting under way. The poetry that ferments and swells and seethes like yeast in the mind must take its time. It defies our haste. The chick in the shell and the vision in the soul have their time to hatch and there is no hurrying them. You cannot run and read—not with poetry.

Poetry is pedestrian. It cannot run on wheels. You take it slow, or not at all. Poetry and speed cannot coexist. The age was choosing between poetry and speed and it was not choosing poetry. The estate of the poet was to fall so low as to threaten disaster to the very friend who had prescribed him, to my great gain, as a substitute for school.

Don Love was running for mayor. I thoughtlessly put it in the paper that he was a reader of Robert Browning, a poet only for highbrows, so my world declared. His campaign manager reproached me through his tears. Though Lincoln was a college town, with professors, students and alumni abounding there, it would never elect a mayor addicted to poetry, least of all that of a Robert Browning whom no one could understand.

To my great relief, Love was elected despite the blot on his 'scutcheon which I had blunderingly exposed. It was a narrow escape, with a special lesson for me. If I was to drink of the poets it must be done in private, with pains to conceal its intoxicant effects. The indulgence in poetry, like any other vice or holiness, is a secret to be kept. The street corner is no place to pray, or to do alms, or to quote poetry. "See thou tell no man" is sound advice now even as nineteen hundred years ago.

With poetry as obsolete as the hoopskirt, I had yet no choice but to take it on. It was the only substitute in sight for the book learning barred from me. My distance vision was good. I could keep comfortably to the open road. I could do the little eyework poetry required. I could find in the poet one minute's reading to keep me thinking for a week. Ten seconds suffice to read and remember:

Humble we must be, if to heaven we go;
High is the roof there, but the gate is low.

All wisdom in nineteen short words! Plant that in my mind and if in a lifetime I have let it grow, I am doing very well.

Keeping it a guilty secret, I took to the road with the poets. I could not carry an encyclopedia, even had I eyes for it. I could put on a slip of paper, and then in my memory, the skylark of a Shelley or the "thing of beauty" of a Keats. The meadowlarks and the landscape and the sunsets were richer in the measure that Keats and Shelley saw farther and felt deeper than I, unaided, could.

The years with the flights of the poets and the walks on the well-worn road went on. At last I was saying with the Prisoner of Chillon: "My very chains and I grew friends." My compulsory walks on the hills and my defensive talks with the poets were no longer a penalty. They were a privilege. Never was a time I could not find in a poet better business for my mind than its own wandering could supply.

All of Rabbi Ben Ezra ("Grow old along with me") I put away in memory—a golden possession for meditative final years. Browning's Saul I stored away, the boy who, trying in vain to save his king, found by his trying (" 'Tis not what a man does

that exalts him, but what he woud do") he had saved himself.
All this and mountains more!

All this was heaping up a fortune I can take with me when
I go. Such luck, those traitor eyes! And I tremble for my country
when I see our speeding time spurn the poet. It was written
of a nation:

Vain was the chief's, the sage's pride!
They had no poet, and they died.

19

A captain of industry

A MAN OF AFFAIRS, protesting some view on an economic matter on which I had rashly editorialized, closed the case by throwing me out of court. I had no right, he said, to an opinion in such matters. I had never met a payroll. It could have been a knock-out blow. I was not knocked out. I had met a payroll. With that fact I sent my critic reeling. I had him on the hip.

I had finished a year of teaching. Of the year's four hundred and fifty dollars salary I had saved just half. Boys brought up on one pair of boots a year and no overcoat need no Ben Franklin to teach them to spend less than they earn. Our later forced-feeding, dollar down economy was yet to come.

My earlier essay as a "prep" at the university had been only an appetizer. I wanted to try again. I looked for a way to make a living as I went. One of the "routes" of the *State Journal*, Lincoln's morning newspaper, was for sale. I bought it for my own two hundred and twenty-five dollars and another two hundred and twenty-five dollars loaned me by Morris Kates, a blessed, reckless, trusting older friend.

A newspaper route was a circulation franchise covering a given area of the town. The franchise holder paid ten cents a week for his papers, delivered them, and collected from his subscriber fifteen. As the city grew, circulation increased, and a profit above the cost of delivery could be made. This profit put a value into the franchise, an "unearned increment." When the route owner, usually a student, graduated and left the city, he looked for a buyer for his route. My four hundred and fifty dollars was the value this one franchise had attained.

My route required two carriers, one horseback, one afoot. I carried the downtown route afoot and enployed a boy with a pony to take the longer suburban route. Every Saturday, without fail, I paid that boy the two dollars and fifty cents he had earned.

I had "met a payroll." Thus I staved off a stigma which might else have hampered me through life. So in that later year I was able to assert my dignity and send my detractor scurrying.

My academic ambition, it turned out, was to be blighted as before. The eyes would not have it. My education, notwithstanding, proceeded prosperously. My paper route opened a new world to me. Many men, it long has been remarked, have grown to a greatness rooted in a newsboy route. My stay was to be too short for anything like that. It was long enough to make friends with a world I should never otherwise have known.

For my papers I paid on Saturday morning sharp. I had to get that income from the customers, that and enough for the payroll and something for myself. Getting it from the customers was the most exacting operation a business man could face. What promptness it took, what diplomacy! A little laxness, a few accounts gone bad and out the profit went. It was a matter of necessity, of stern principle, to drag in every dime. I would walk a mile for a laggard customer's fifteen cents. If he put me off today, I was back, another mile, tomorrow.

Here was life as it was lived in the homes of my common folk customers. I saw the "lives of quiet desperation" which Henry Thoreau had marked. I saw how strictly honorable most people were, how reprobate some could be. The weekly fifteen cents was for most of my customers endurable, while sixty-five cents a month would be impossible. I had to be there on Saturday morning. If I delayed till Monday, the fifteen cents put by on the clock shelf would be gone for something else.

The Burlington paid its men monthly, each 13th. I must collect monthly. If I was at the door on the 14th the sixty-five cents was mine. If I was tardy, another month, and maybe forever, was to wait. One man, when I came to his office with my bill for a monthly sixty-five cents, invariably gave me a half dollar, never more. He died owing me a dozen delinquent fifteen cents!

I had to be up and out at four a.m. By that experience I gained a lifetime sympathy for all people compelled to get up early in the morning. To be able, even though poor, to have my sleep out in the morning has been, ever since, my standard of luxury. But once out and afoot at four o'clock, what fun! Through rain or snow or zero cold it was all the same, a joy. Weather, to a healthy youth pounding the pavements before daylight, keeping his fingers warm by rolling his papers, has no terrors, can be dismissed.

The people met on these morning rounds, never to be known again! The all-night drunks staggering to their holes, weary, bleary, in hell before their time. The hag down in the danger district who gave me a dollar. Bring me, she said, something good to read. She never went up town herself. A brand to be plucked from the burning, thought I in my innocence. I bought an *Atlantic Monthly* and a *Harper's Bazaar* and a *Ladies' Home Journal* and left them at her door.

When I came on Saturday to collect for the paper the gratitude I looked for was a raging bitterness. What she had wanted, she stormed, was something like the *Police Gazette*!

A year of this. I had met the payroll, balanced the budget, made my living and paid the debt to Morris Kates. *Journal* routes were booming. I sold mine for eight hundred and fifty dollars and turned to other fields. Who could say that I was not a successful businessman, as such entitled to hold opinions of my own? Possessed, moreover, of an education in a world no man can wisely miss.

20

Key to politics

In 1890 the Democrats of the First Nebraska District nominated for Congress a young, unknown Lincoln lawyer, lately from Jacksonville, Illinois. He had asked for the nomination, not expecting election, to help him get started in his practice of law.

In Nebraska in those days Democrats did not run for office to win. The state was settled largely by Civil War veterans who voted "as they shot." Democrats were "copperheads." The offices were mostly reserved for veterans. A Democratic nomination, in the eyes of a majority, was not even a compliment. The young lawyer from Lincoln leaped into the fray with fire in his eye and silver on his tongue. When the votes were counted, William Jennings Bryan was famous. To the universal amazement, he was in.

Country boys, in those days, kept close to home. No jalopies of course, nor even bicycles, tempted them to tour. I lived only a dozen miles from the capital, yet I had never seen a governor or a congressman—no personality and power more imposing than Pat Lyman, awesome autocrat of our local passenger train. I had contemplated the dimensions of greatness, as when the boy in McGuffey raised the question:

> How big was Alexander, Pa,
> That people called him great?

And of course I knew the dimensions of the giant whom David slew with a pebble from the brook. Goliath towered a full "six cubits and a span," which I figured at not less than nine feet tall. Could a congressman, a stateman, be less? When word went 'round that Congressman Bryan, the new star in the sky, was to speak at Hickman four miles away, I hurried down to see for myself how big Alexander the Great might be.

In Nathaniel Hawthorne's story of The Great Stone Face the people of a valley look for a man to come whose countenance should match for majesty a face carved by nature on the mountain wall above. Famous men, statesmen and generals presented themselves. The people gazed in hope, then shook their heads. Alas! The man to match the mountain could not be found. Even so, there I waited, watching for the man big enough to be a congressman.

The people about me were strangers, but mortal men of the form and manner familiar to me. None of these could be the congressman. I started a bit when a pompous little man with a heavy watch chain and a projecting abdomen came in; but no, he would not do. Other men of goodly grace appeared. However tall, they were not big enough. Then through a side door a man stepped in quietly and my heart leaped up assured. There was the man, and no mistake.

William Jennings Bryan, in his early thirties, was an Apollo of a man. His body was only that of any well proportioned man, yet he filled and overflowed the room. The confident poise, the gravity, the lightning in his eye, the benign face, the wide, firm mouth combined into a commanding, appealing personality. Add the rhythm of his words and the music of his voice and you had the man who, a little later, was to take a national convention by storm and win, before his course was run, three nominations for president.

No mortal could be as great as, to my untutored eyes, the young congressman that night appeared. The usual disillusionment lay ahead. Politics is not at all the romance a young lad may dream. But from that hour, stirred by a mighty man of politics, I was to be exploring and pondering the world of politics for myself. I had taken for granted, till that time, that politics, for me, was merely to vote for the Democrats and hoot at the Republicans. Soon I made a staggering discovery. Among the services rendered by the parties was that of packing into pigeonholes such voters as I had planned to be, in effect disfranchising them. Here, as in Washington, we were a government of balanced powers, pigeonhole versus pigeonhole.

Democracy gives votes alike to Simple Simon and to Socrates. Simple Simon could not run a government. He would ruin it. What to do with him? Simple as Simon! Such as refuse to labor in their minds with politics automatically range themselves about equally in the two opposing pigeonholes. There, with their unvarying voting, they cancel each other out. They make themselves harmless ballast in the hold of the ship of state. I decided to be, not ballast, but a balancer. I would take whichever side of the ship of state needed my weight to restore a balance in danger of being lost. I called that, and still call it, being independent, a liberal.

I walk on two legs. Once erect on one foot, I begin a forward fall. I am out of balance. Time then for the other foot to intervene, restore the balance, press on the forward pace. So with peoples and their politics. From the Civil War on our balance was being lost. One set of interests too long and far held sway. The farmers of the plains and the laborers in the mills were neglected, suffering. There was corruption, monopoly, special privilege. It was time for the other "foot" to assert itself, restore the balance lost. The needed revolt was stirring at the grassroots then. The Bryan I saw rising so swiftly was its product, its voice, not its cause. Many another potent name was to figure in the years ahead in the drive to restore the balance, insert the saving other foot.

Two men, in the year of my first vote, personified the new look then appearing in politics. One was my neighbor, Bryan, leading the uprising against the "interests" then long in control of the government. The other was Mark Hanna, with brilliant skill rallying the defense.

The eloquence of Bryan was setting the prairies afire. He menaced the prevailing powers with a massive grassroots vote. Mark Hanna (the Democrats called him "Dollar" Mark) applied to politics the organizing genius of the big businessman. He made money count, as never before, in mobilizing votes.

Hanna, in 1896, fought hard and won easily. The political extinction of Bryan was proclaimed. The conflict was not so quickly to be quelled. Bryan entitled his book on the '96 campaign "The First Battle." It was not, of course, the first. Such battles had been going on from the time of Thomas Jefferson.

And it was not to be the last. The essence of the Bryan-Hanna conflict, with changing forms, has been unceasing from the beginning of our government. It is inherent in all governments.

Here is the unending struggle, the subject of all our politics: to keep in balance the powers on which our issues turn. The Fathers provided balanced powers within the government. Knowing how power corrupts its possessor and enslaves its subjects, they saw to it that no department of the government should have an unchecked sway. It was left to the people, to their politics, to keep an equal balance among themselves. Let any man, section, class, or party gain unchecked power and our liberties, no matter what our form of government, are lost.

Whatever form and confusion our politics assumes, the substance is the same. Does any person, group or interest wield an overweening and therefore dangerous power over us? Then it is for politics to check that power, restore the lost balance, put the ship again on even keel. Out of such an effort to restore a balance was our nation born. Power, in the mother country, had grown arrogant. It exploited its colonies. There seemed no way to restore the balance by peaceful votes and so we went to war. By that costly means, balance, as between two nations, was restored.

Once free from outside control, the problem of the balance within remained. Only by keeping our sections, classes, interests in equilibrium could liberty with order be maintained. Lose that balance, as we did in 1861, and calamity comes. This makes the preoccupation, as James Madison expected, of our politics.

There is a rhythm, as I think our history shows, in the nation's life and politics. "We walk a mile, we rest awhile," as the old song goes. There is a period of placidity when the people are quiescent, or content. During that period, abuses and injustices appear. As fleas gravitate to a sleeping dog and barnacles to an anchored ship, so corruption and privilege creep into the place of power, subtly seizing it.

Then the ship must be debarnacled. The dog snaps at his fleas. The period of calm is followed by a storm. Thus politics goes by fits and starts. Following the domination of the conservative Hamilton had come the revolt with Thomas Jefferson.

Years of quiet, then, and a new uprising brought Andrew Jackson to the scene. A quarter of a century passed, then Lincoln came.

In 1896 there had been a thirty year period of power, with mounting abuses on the way. Here came Bryan and the Populists, marching in revolt. Bryan was swamped. It was only the "first battle." The fighting went right on.

Theodore Roosevelt, among the Republicans, took up his "big stick" and joined the fray. His party, on that issue, was to break in two. Woodrow Wilson carried on for the Democrats. The nation had been thirty years falling out of balance. To get the people back to their "born equal" state was to take the next thirty years.

The "power of the people" was to be shored up with direct primaries, income and inheritance taxes, direct election of senators, votes for women, social security, labor unions. Mark Hanna, who had won in '96, was beaten in the end.

So has gone, through my years, the way of change, of what we hope is progress. The simple key to all this? The proper process and purpose of politics is to keep power in leash, to keep our powers diverse and in balance—the way to a government serving the one proper aim of government, a shelter for free men.

21

The journalistic sea

DR. CASEY WOOD, in Chicago, put my eyes through their paces and shook his head. Get a job as a seaman, he said—I could live on the sea without strain or pain, but print my eyes would never stand.

It was trouble with his eyes, Dr. Wood recalled, led Richard Henry Dana to make the voyage which fruited in "Two Years Before the Mast," a book which everyone, in that day, read. I could be a sailor, even if not author of a great book. Or a farmer, the good doctor said comfortingly, presenting his bill for twenty-five dollars.

Back in Lincoln with the great doctor's decision and advice I walked into the office of Joseph C. Seacrest, *State Journal* publisher, with whom I had gained a nodding acquaintance while running a *Journal* route.

"You ought," I said, "to be publishing a farm paper. You have the plant. This is a farmer state. It's an opportunity." He would think about it, he said.

"JC," as everyone called him, became a newspaper publisher by a route wide open then and steadily closing since. He had come a few years before from Pennsylvania with empty pockets and full of nerve energy. He found a job with an evening paper.

Evening papers in those days were as easy to start and about as plentiful and ephemeral as restaurants. A few fonts of type, a flat-bed press and you were an editor and publisher. It was not long till venturesome Seacrest had a paper of his own. In due time he combined his evening paper with the morning *Journal*, he publisher of both. Such things bold men could do in the days when a daily could be bought for the price of a modern Cadillac. It was, for him, a tiny plunge I had challenged "JC" to make.

He phoned me, a couple of days later, to come on over. He had decided to do it, he said. He would start a weekly farm paper, the *Independent Farmer*. What was my interest in the thing?

"I want to edit it," I said.

"All right," he replied, "how about eighteen dollars a week?"

I had an ambition, I said, to make a thousand dollars a year. He scratched a minute on a pad. "That will be nineteen dollars and twenty cents a week. We'll start March 1," he said.

A fig for Dr. Casey Wood! I was going to sea, the sea I had longed for all my days, the stormy, rock-bound, shark infested, glory-girdled journalistic sea.

Three beautiful spring months went by. Another summons from the publisher. "Your paper's no go. We've thrown it out of the window," he said.

I reached for my hat. He raised a restraining hand. "We never fire anyone," he said. "Go up and see Will Jones, the managing editor." I was suddenly a writer of editorials, soon with the imposing title of associate editor. A world had opened up which I was to be exploring through all my working years.

I was burning to be, on the smaller scale my talents might allow, a Horace Greeley, a Henry Watterson. I did not know that the Greeleys and the Wattersons had already gone the way of the passenger pigeon, the one-hoss shay. The newspaper, as I did not know, had grown too big to be a one-man show.

The editor, in the days then ending, was a fighting man. He spent his life on the firing line of politics. Most newspapers existed, in those days, for political purposes and by grace of politics. The editor framed the fiery phrases by which his party was to win the county offices, the legislative seats, the governorship. He was a central figure in the public eye. He lived dangerously. He might at any time be horsewhipped by an enraged opposing partisan. Now and then he was shot at by a candidate he had hounded to defeat.

It was a fast, furious and famous life. There was romance in it. His life was a battle, and the newspaper was the lengthened shadow of the editor. What wonder a boy who had been a good speller and knew the difference between subject and predicate should look with awe and yearning on the embattled editor with thousands hanging on his printed word.

In dimension, it was, to tell the truth, a small world to which I aspired. Daily newspapers, in that day, were for the few. Only five men received daily papers in Roca village when I was there as a boy: the precinct Republican leader, Robert Haroop, Dr. Demaree, Storekeeper Bendlage, William Charlton, the stockman, and W. E. Keys, who owned the quarry. But they were a potent five. Through them the might of the editor was reflected to the unreading rest of us. Not even John L. Sullivan, that day's phenomenon of the fists, received more reverent respect than Samuel Bowles, master of the all-important Springfield *Republican*.

Such was the world that was vanishing when I so expectantly entered it. The common measure of the change the times have brought is from the horse and buggy to the rocket plane. Not less portentous has been the change from the giant editor of my youth to the giant journal of today.

Managing Editor Will Owen Jones saw the new world coming and told me so when Publisher Seacrest of the *Journal* so humanely sent me upstairs. The newspaper, he said, was getting too big a dog for the party tail to wag. The news, not politics, was to be the proper subject of the press. The subscriber and the advertiser, not the spoils of politics, were to be the source and support of the newspaper to come. Rural free delivery, long opposed as a socialist scheme, was at last here. With it came the penny press. A daily could be had for a year for little more than a weekly had cost before. To reach down to the new readers the "yellow press" appeared.

New departments—sports, comics, society—were added to hold the wider readership. This meant bigger, faster presses, more typesetting machines, more building space—more capital. In Lincoln, the *Evening Call* and the starveling *Democratic Post* grew pale and wan and died. The newspaper deaths and consolidations which have marked the years since got swiftly under way.

The day of fewer, bigger things had come to the press as to other fields. The colossus in the rowboat is but a speck in the crowd that makes the ocean liner go. The one-man show was done. I was to be fifty years an editor without once being held important enough to be shot at, or to suffer a blackened eye or

broken nose. So ended, in the field of news and opinion, an old
world. So came a new.

I came just in time to be in at the death of a journalistic age,
the day of small things, with much that was scandalous, irre-
sponsible, mean; and much that was brilliant, good. The day of
fewer, but more solvent journals was advancing steadily, with
doubts and dangers of its own, through all my fifty-odd
journalistic years.

Was not the press, nonetheless, once I was a part of it, to fix
all things up, make all things right? What of the noble rhyme
of Joseph Story which all of us used to quote:

> *Here shall the press the people's right maintain,*
> *Unaw'd by influence and unbrib'd by gain;*
> *Here patriot Truth her glorious precepts draw,*
> *Pledged to Religion, Liberty, and Law.*

I had waited for Anna Ord to clear up her desk and go home
so I could sweep out the schoolhouse and go home myself. When
in school I was deep in Barnes' *Fourteen Weeks* in history and
was satisfied with what I saw. America was all right and wonderful. I said as much to Anna Ord. Some things needed fixing,
she said, shaking the chalk dust out of her jacket as she put
it on to go.

I had no way of knowing then that school history books are
not given to showing the seamier side of things. Our history
must make patriots, no less than scholars, of us. Aside from the
fact that too many Republicans held the public offices, I knew
of nothing greatly needing fixing up. If anything, anyway, were
wrong, it could be fixed up as soon as I grew up and got to work
on it. My plan to fix such things as might be out of order had
something to do, I suppose, with my unceasing itch to write.

The close of the old century brought the rise of that gaudy
journalistic nauseousness, the "yellow press." Off went the bloom
from my Joseph Story dream. But that, too, could be fixed when
I got around to it. So now when Publisher Seacrest kicked me
upstairs to write editorials, to tell the world what was what, I
felt that the world and I were on our way. The years since the
boyhood talk with Anna Ord had confirmed her view, rather

than my own. Many things needed fixing. Well, what was I
there for, anyway?

The fields, for the would-be straightener out of things, were
white for the harvest as the new century dawned. The corporate
powers (labor and agriculture still innocently unorganized) had
had free hand. What that hand had found to do, it had done with
all its might. Trusts were spawning out of Delaware like eels
in the Sargasso sea. Greed was gutting our natural wealth.
Political machines were the property of special interests. The
people were taking what the "bosses" handed out to them. In
my simplicity I had taken seriously Thomas Jefferson, the Democratic party saint, and Abraham Lincoln, the Republican frontis-
piece. As a son of the state which proclaimed that mountaineers
are always free men, I took government by the people for granted.
Seeing what was going on, I took my pen in hand.

We began, there in Nebraska, on the party nominating machinery. The party nominating convention was a perfect device
for keeping the people in bounds. The machines shot their slates
through these conventions with supernal skill. Government by
the people consisted of a choice between the pickings of the
two machines.

When the fight was over, the direct primary had succeeded
the convention in Nebraska and in most of the other states.
Government "by the people" seemed to have won a sweeping
victory.

There remained the senators. The legislatures, till then,
named the senators. Who really named the senators? When the
results appeared, the Burlington had named the Nebraska South-
Platte senator, the Union Pacific the North-of-the-Platte senator.
The Senate in Washington, the maneuvering in the legislatures
done, had become the "millionaires' club." We went on, the
nation agreeing, to popular election of senators. We even went
on to direct legislation, the initiative and referendum.

All this, with my approval, half a century ago. The power of
the people to fix things up was settled. Now for the millenium!

In helping enlarge the power of the people I still think I
was right. In my expectations of a prompt Utopia I was, of
course, wrong. The struggle for government "by the people,"

as I should have known, but clears the way for a greater struggle following. Government by the people cannot be better or wiser than the people, its source. Hardly half of us vote in elections; fewer still employ their power in the primary. Demos and Plutus compete in schemes to mislead us. The rise into larger wisdom for ourselves goes on, but slow. We cannot gather figs from thistles, knowledge from ignorance, virtue from venality.

Laid aside is my dream of getting the world fixed up while yet I am here to attend to it. That means getting ourselves fixed up. This takes more time than I had counted on. Will our new atomic powers grant us the time it takes?

22

I run away

THE LUSITANIA HAD BEEN SUNK. Europe was weltering in war and the fire was edging our way. The President was writing protesting notes which were having no effect. A cloud larger than the sky was hanging over us.

The world, that day in May, 1916, was too much for me. I boarded the morning train from Lincoln to South Bend, on the Platte an hour away. Thence, taking the day for it, I would follow the river to Ashland, fifteen miles away, thence home by rail at supper time. Moses took forty years in the desert to summon the spirit to defy old Pharaoh. Surely I could take one day away to fit me for a fierce-faced world.

I was met at the South Bend station by a stranger with sharp voice and yellow vest. But for the vest I could have taken him for an old boyhood friend, one I had much admired. No fighter myself, I the more adored a short-tempered, unterrified little bird with a white tip to its tail. The kingbird would fight its weight in wildcats. Many a time had I stood below and cheered it on as it chased a crow or hawk across the sky. The day was too sunny, too sweet, to be spoiled by thought of my inconsistency. But there I was, honoring the belligerent kingbird and running from a fight.

But for his yellow vest and the stripe at the side, not tip of his tail, I should have confused the fellow who greeted me with my old fighting friend. I would not have been far wrong. This was a cousin of my kingbird friend, the rarer Arkansas breed. I wrote him first in the list of the fifty friends who were to be in line to greet me as the day went on. Spoke up the older friend, perched on a fence beside the road, ere I could write the new friend down. The blue jays, of course, were immediately there with copious comments, a scratchy pencil on a slate or a squeaky horse trough pump.

A phoebe called its name at the bridge it was claiming for a home. The robins were all around. A village like South Bend, the robins plainly suppose, is made especially for them. They strut about with an owner's air, grudgingly giving way when a mere man comes by. Even a quiet village is too much world for a world-weary wanderer on such a day as this. A wren calls and a cardinal clicks and a downy woodpecker pokes at his tree, but I hasten forth impatient to be alone.

Alone? No sooner was I clear of the town and its sniffing dogs than I was peering in every nook and cranny for company. To be alone would have left me with myself for company. I would be on that day no good company. I would surely be taking along the world I was hurrying to escape. Somewhere in the willows by the river a prothonotary warbler surely could be found. A bashful fellow, his royal yellowness is worth long miles to meet. Seeking solitude, I yearned for that bird's company.

I parted the willows. I wet my feet. Many a red-wing blackbird rewarded me. Coots by the dozen with their white noses came. (God must love the coots; he makes so many of them.) A bittern flew up and a blue-winged teal. An eared grebe dove at sight of me, arousing old-time baffled memories. How often, as a rabbit-hunting boy, I had shot at him. He would dive at the flash of fire, safe from the shot to follow it. Then he would pop up beyond my gun's reach, to make a nose at me. So much less blood on my hands today!

So seeking the yearned-for warbler I spied a spoonbill duck and a Louisiana water thrush and a muskrat and a spotted sandpiper and a short-billed marsh wren. Never a prothonotary warbler was I to see till another day at another place when the war had been fought and won and the peace, by men's bungling, forfeited. I climbed the bluff above the stream and the railroad track beside it, pursuing a meadowlark. A man appeared. I had come to escape all men.

But he was not of this world, this man. The *Lusitania* was nothing to him. He was planting corn beneath the sky and that was the world to him. I inquired politely: Was I likely to find a prairie chicken thereabouts? Where was my gun? he asked. I had only my binoculars. I merely wanted to look at him, I said.

He looked at me, incredulous, and clucked to his horses. Men with guns, he said, had killed off the prairie chickens years ago. Now they were out killing each other off.

So the world of guns pursued me still. He went in one direction with his plow. I fled the other way. I could not find a prothonotary warbler. A grasshopper sparrow, then?

Dr. Robert Walcott, the biologist, when his students at the university weighed too heavily upon him, sought sanity among the birds. All the infinite things I was never to learn about the birds, Bob Walcott knew. I had learned from him to know a grasshopper sparrow by his grasshopper voice. I determined that day, as I walked, to spy the sparrow which I had only heard.

Seeking the grasshopper sparrow I found the plaintive Harris sparrow, scores of him, and the field sparrow, lark sparrow, chipping sparrow, Savannah sparrow, song sparrow, tree sparrow. I was the man in the fable who dug for gold and got no gold but, what was better, good crops of things which nourished him as gold could never do.

The sun descended and I bagged an indigo bunting, and divers warblers, and noted how well the sweet clover grew on the sterile railroad cuts. Then out from that world of sky and birds and stream I came, born again, to the railroad train and home, ready for any world.

How one day afoot on the open road, under an open sky, can stand forth bright against a cloud of unimpressive after-years! At home that night I wrote, and the next day printed, the story of this runaway. That was my beginning as a columnist.

23

Progress and its pains

THERE HAD BEEN A STRIKE in the Roca quarry just before I came there in 1884. The twelve-hour day had been shortened to eleven, yet there was discontent. Led by an agitator I shall call Bill Burns, the men laid down their wheelbarrows, shovels, crowbars, picks and sledges and demanded a ten-hour day. As the story was told, William E. Keys, the proprietor, said simply to Milton McKinnon, the foreman, when the demand was made: "Fire Bill Burns and give in to the rest." So the strike and Bill Burns were ended.

In the year I was born, saintly Henry Ward Beecher, the nation's outstanding pulpit orator, was denouncing trade unions. They were socialism, he said. The country needed cheap labor. He approved President Hayes' veto of a Chinese exclusion bill. The competition of the swarming Chinese would keep labor in its place. The worker who could not live on a dollar a day did not deserve to live. Fifteen years later I was working as a section hand for a dollar and fifteen cents a day and saving the fifteen cents for a rainy day. The "coddling" of labor had begun.

When the railroad strikes of the late Seventies came, consternation filled the land. Such a strike was rebellion against the government. A delegation of locomotive engineers protested a cut of ten per cent in pay. The members of the committee were fired, just like Bill Burns. Served them right, good people said. When the farmers objected to eating forever at the second table, it was as if Oliver had "asked for more." Farmers were to farm, not fret, shuddered scandalized solid citizens.

When farm laborers set fire to the new harvesting machinery which took their jobs away our cup of woe was full. The country was going to the mobs. Such were the minds and times when I was awakening to my world.

When panic-stricken governors of states called for federal troops to cope with the railroad strikes, President Hayes yielded and sent the soldiers. But in doing so he suggested a question too radical then for public view. If railroad workers were to be regulated by force of government, should not the employers likewise be controlled? So asked, under his breath, that conservative president.

For minds were moving with the new machines. Our bodies were to speed up, in my one life, from a horse trot to the flight of sound—and more. Could our brains keep up with them?

The telephone and I were born together. The railroads were still in their first half century. The new machines took over the old jobs. They lightened labor and heightened speed and we gloried in them as they came. But the minds to put the new giants, steam and electricity, in their place, to keep them from binding the people they had the power to emancipate—there was the problem. Machines change fast. Minds move slow. From the first crow-hop flight of the Wrights in America to aerial navies in Europe sending down their "ghastly dew" was but a dozen years. The human mind had not been geared to such a dizzy speed.

In my West Virginia youth men rode their saw-logs to market down swollen streams, saved from ducking and drowning by stepping fast from log to log. Now came a world of swollen streams with footing fleeting as whirling logs. Could mind keep pace with feet to keep the balance we must have or drown?

I was born to a time which, as between Darwin and the devil, had little preference. Hardly anyone worries about evolution now. It was heresy, in 1875, to lay government hands on the railroads, first of the monster machines. Thirty years later that heresy was orthodox.

The labor union, in Henry Ward Beecher's 1875, was a subversive enterprise. Labor unions, with their tens of millions of members, are valued as indispensable to the balance which keeps the economy on even keel today.

The farmer, in 1875, was well flattered by the politicians; but as lately as the 1920's, presidents, indignant at his demands for equality with other interests, were vetoing the bills for his "relief." Now he has, at least in theory, his "parity." He is one of the equal legs of the stool on which we poise our industry.

Susan B. Anthony, in 1875, was arguing that the men who had nobly freed and enfranchised the slaves should give the free women liberty to vote. They arrested her as a subversive character! Now the women have been voting for more than thirty years.

Our country, in 1875, was all the world we cared for. We hid from the rest behind God's oceans and our man-made tariff walls. Here we are now, out in front, knowing the world as one. These years of mental surgery (there is no anesthetic for operations on the mind) it has been my lot to view. Thus have our slow minds been tortured and strained by the swift machines our own hands have imposed on them. So the times have changed since, in the 1850s, Grandfather Shields and his brother-in-law, Elias Nichols, had their line-fence falling out. Their farms adjoined, each with its hill-top house. A hollow lay between. Surveying in those days was informal, tree to tree and rock to rock. Differences over boundaries easily arose.

The Shields-Nichols dispute was carried into the church for settlement. The result was, as told to me long afterward, that my grandfather was expelled from the church. That, if you prized your immortal soul, was then a drastic penalty. Such was the simple justice of that simple time and place. By the time my memory began, a relenting church had taken my forgiving grandfather back, but the breach in the family, the old feud, remained. The Nichols home, with my grandmother's sister presiding there, showed near and clear from my grandmother's house, but I was never to enter it.

Years later my Uncle John was involved in a like dispute. The times had changed. This dispute was settled, not in the church down by McKim, but in the court at the county seat. Justice had become by now a secular commodity at a price. When I visited him afterward, Uncle John told me sadly that when his trouble arose he had scraped together a fortune, a full five hundred dollars of his own.

When the day in court was done, gone was the fortune, too.

The world of men was waning. The world of machines, of less than human things was coming on apace. The new century brought the first billion dollar corporation, Steel. Arriving in

Nebraska, I found forces looming there such as had been unknown, or at least invisible, in the West Virginia hills. The
railroads, the packers, the grain companies, the lumber "trust"
were powers with which the old time ways were ill-equipped to
cope. Corporate giant overshadowed midget man.

On the open road Walt Whitman had celebrated the free and
simple life. I was to be rich by the fewness of my wants. I could
squat by some pond like Walden and be, like David Thoreau,
a king. No man could master me. I could be my sovereign self.
Here came Old Walt, yawping (his own word) of the glory of
being just a man. He would love all men as brothers, but if they
did not love him, Walt would still be Walt. I could be what I
pleased for aught of him. It would be all the same with Walt.
"Resist much, obey little," he rebelliously advised his countrymen.

Walt, for all his defiance of exterior control, was the most
sociable of men. He would love to go along with you, but never
would he cringe. He had his dream of a city "invincible to the
attacks of the whole of the rest of the earth." Would that not be
a regimented city then, its men defending it in solid rank, no
liberty? Heavens, no! It was to be invincible because all its folk
were friends. There would be peace and order and justice, but
only because everyone there was ruled by "robust love." (Hadn't
John of Patmos, a previous poet, reported a city of the sort?)

No, nothing corporate, "nothing external," could quell Walt
Whitman, proclaimer of himself and of free men everywhere.
Abraham Lincoln, another adviser on the road, was, unlike these
others, a practical man. He had come, by some freak of national
good fortune, to be president. He had done a magnificent job. He,
too, was of the cabin breed which held that a man, to be a man,
must be free. He would no more be slaveholder than a slave.
The goverment "of" the people must be "by" the people.

Now in my day was coming on, headlong, the revolution
which the machines were hurrying. The machines men made
to free their bodies seemed bent on binding their souls. To muster
the strength to own and control so great a machine as a railroad,
oil company or mine, men had to merge themselves. They combined in corporations. The machines of iron must be manned by
machines of flesh.

The single worker, helpless before the corporate employer, was moved to incorporate himself. The labor machine arose to balance the capital machine. The reluctant farmers, last of men to yield their individual liberty, were forced, in self defense, to follow suit. In Congress the "farm bloc" arose. Finally, to keep itself sovereign in the presence of these proud private powers, "big government" appeared.

Two mighty revolutions have thus come together and opposed each other through all my times. There has been that conclusive, irresistible rising to new power of "the people" which has marked, from its beginning, our nation's life. Since I helped Silas McHenry "buck" staves in the West Virginia woods the speed of that movement has multiplied. There has come a broadened suffrage, more popular control of politics, more service by government to the many, not merely, as of old, to a few. Meanwhile, this other revolution: this gathering of private men into bodies corporate—business, labor, profession, everything. As men become more mere parts of a "machine," they tend to grow less as men. The one revolution tends to bind the man the other frees.

This turning of my world from man to machine was getting on my nerves. I took to the Fortieth Street Road to dream of preserving liberty. Was man to be ground up in the machines which he himself had made? That was forty years ago, before Hitler and Stalin with their monster machines had done their bloody work. I would have been yet more troubled had I seen the years ahead.

It had been as natural for a western editor to rail at the trusts as for my dog Haze to snap at fleas. The so-called trusts, despite our railings and the laws our railings wrote, had rolled resistlessly on. Their power to grind out food and raiment and all the things our comfort required had lulled the fear of their turning to grinding men. We could not stop them. What was to do but join them? We must all incorporate. Labor formed its unions. The farmers formed their cooperatives, their blocs. Doctors, lawyers, teachers, actors, writers took refuge in their guilds. We were now to be members as well as men. We were to speak and write and vote, not as a weak, isolated "I," but a powerful incorporated "we."

Such has been the revolution of my age—the change from "I" to "we." Both war and wealth have decreed it. Even in the woods of West Virginia the cross-cut saw was a two-man job. It took a dozen for the raising of a house. It was not good for man to be alone. But the question stays, the eternal question of the coming years: How assure, with our corporate body, the freedom of our lone soul?

There was government, of course, in my boyhood hills, but you had to hunt to find it. In my nine years there I never saw a policeman. Government was for the few criminals, not for the rest of us. When Town Marshal Oliver Hile ordered me off the Roca sidewalk with my wheelbarrow, that was my first contact with government, the law. A little later, in the city for a day, I came upon a Roca boy who had moved to the big town. We stood at a corner talking quietly. A policeman coming by told us roughly to move on. That was my first taste of the "police state." I did not like it then. I do not like it now. "The meanest man on the force," my friend said, thus early become an enemy of the "state."

Once a year there were taxes to pay at the courthouse. Such tiny taxes! The roads we made ourselves. Two days a year each voter was called forth to work out his "road tax" by the labor of his horses and his hands. Such roads! The school tax was the largest item in our tax bill, and that was levied by ourselves in free town-meeting way. County and state had so little to do, the cost of running them was small.

Then came the age of speed, the age of big things, the corporate age, and with it the omnipresent government. When the first traffic light was hung over O street, Lincoln's main thoroughfare, the West Virginia freeman (*Montani semper liberi!*) was scandalized. Government telling us when to start, when stop? What of our liberties?

I wrote and the paper printed a satirical story of two citizens who set out to travel from the railway station to the old Lindell hotel. Not to waste their lives while waiting for the new traffic lights to change, they carried a table with them. When the light ahead glared red, they would set the table down and play a game of checkers to while away the wait. Thus, we said, thanks to the

new traffic lights, two checker champions were born. I received
many grateful notes from impatient, obstructed citizens. The
traffic lights meanwhile stayed and multiplied. They had to.

The street traffic problem with its resulting big government
was a minor matter compared with the traffic on the rails. If we
had had little government by the government, there had been
plenty by the public utilities. The railroads, with their trans-
portation monopoly, held our welfare in their hands. They could
decree, by their rates and rebates, which communities, industries
and individuals should thrive. They created grain monopolies
and took command of our politics. That was too much power
for private interests to wield.

Now look at us! I had been a Jeffersonian Democrat, holding
that the best government was the government that governed
least. I still resented Oliver Hile, ordering me and my wheelbarrow off the sidewalk. And now I was calling for more government, bigger government, to keep these private powers in their
place.

That has been my dilemma, and that of millions like me,
through all this half century. Knowing that only the freeman is
fully a man, we want the greatest possible liberty for everyone.
We know from history that the more government there is, the
less liberty there is apt to be. Yet we have supported measure
after measure to increase the power and scope of government.
We have put government to regulating public utilities, to over-
seeing banks and stock exchanges, to inspecting food and drugs
and newspaper ownership and pretending to limit political campaign funds. We put government to lending money to businessmen and home buyers. Government sets up unemployment in-
surance, old age pensions, "social security."

All this "big government" I, who dread and suspect big government, have advocated and approved. The thing that I would
not, that I do. All for good and sufficient reason. For we were
not choosing between big government and little government.
We were choosing between public big government and private
big government.

The age of the economic mammoth, product of the rise of
the machine, an age capable of being beneficent, had come. Here

were private powers too great to go unchecked. In the hills, making our own molasses, grinding our own grain, we depended only on ourselves. If we cheated, we cheated ourselves. Now for our every necessity we depended on public utilities, on stores, on factories. When one man depends on another, government must step in. Either one man governs another, or government governs both.

Through all these decades we have been choosing between two dangers, between private government in which we have no control, and public government in which we have a vote. Fearing them both, we have been preferring the risks of public government. Fifty years of this and I, who lived my first ten years without feeling a finger of government, find government supervising every turn I make. Only by its permission may I drive my car. Wherever I go, a highway patrolman is breathing down my neck. Imperiously, the divers governments which tax me command me to their feet, had in hand, to defend a tax return. Life for the businessman is one long reporting and explaining this or that to some demanding instrument of government.

We have risked big public government to save ourselves from private tyranny. But government itself, as other countries and certain tendencies in our own reveal, can be the most hideous of tyrannies. I was to spend my life devoted to little government and consenting to more and more big government. Big government, in this new world, was the "least possible" government.

Now the worst was yet to come. Government had been hitherto our own American government. Now we must join the rest of the world in a common, universal government. It is that or be consumed in the fires of relentless war. We had had our own little brush with Spain, a war pressed on us, so we thought, by outside forces we could not control. Japan and Russia, a little later, were at each other's throats. The Kaiser was rattling his sword in Europe.

A bitter fact was coming clear. A world of unchecked sovereign nations meant a world forever dragged into war. Any warlike state, at its own will, could plunge the most peaceful nation into war. Not even isolated America could be safe. Where then was our sovereignty, our liberty? When Theodore Roosevelt and William H. Taft and other conservative leaders laid a plan for a "League to Enforce Peace," this meant yet more government, but I gladly followed them. What less could a sane man do?

Right then the Kaiser launched his war and the fire was reaching us. We would fight this time, yes, but this war must end war. The war won, Woodrow Wilson came back from Versailles with his League of Nations to enforce the peace. More government, but indispensable government.

The world, since Calvary, has seen no sadder sight than followed then. Men's minds, at any given time, are as they are. They cannot quickly change. Powerful men, to serve purposes of their own, were able to rally old minds against the new hope. The League, in the Senate, went down. The "next war," the path thus cleared for it, came remorselessly on.

On a morning in Miami when that second war was done I stood, with others, face to face with Winston Churchill, a monumental hero of that war. I had a question to put to him: "With the United States in the League of Nations, would this second war have been prevented?" He answered with one emphatic word: "Yes."

Contritely we moved, after this war we could have prevented, to set up the United Nations, a new League. One more effort through government, more government, to keep the world at peace! I am still for the more government. The alternative is too terrible. We must take the chance—the chance that monster government may be seized by monstrous men, as a Hitler in Germany, a Stalin in Russia. We are then in a trap which we ourselves of our own free will have made.

Men bent on being free have their gift of freedom even in prison cells. Such men, if, happily, there be enough of us, will yet make our corporate age their fruitful servant, not their despoiling lord. My dream that November day of forty years ago on the Fortieth Street Road has often since been dimmed, but never dashed. To let it be dashed is death.

24

Just a man or two

DON LOVE SAID: "If you're going to spend your days on the open road afoot, you should take Thoreau along." Just then B. Fay Mills came to town preaching the gospel of a carpenter named Whitman. Walt Whitman had been dismissed from a government clerkship fifty years before because of a book of poems which he composed. Whitman had died unpopular and virtually a pauper in 1892. Now he was buried gold. People were quoting his poems, especially "The Open Road." That pointed in my direction. With David Thoreau's *Walden* I took *Leaves of Grass* as well.

Another name, not much exalted when I was born, was taking on luster in the new century. A life of Abraham Lincoln by Ida Tarbell was much talked about. My Irish grandfather in West Virginia had been consigned, as I have told before, to the military prison at Columbus, Ohio, for imprudently hurrahing for Jeff Davis when Abraham Lincoln's soldiers were around. His Pennsylvania Dutch wife, my gentle grandmother, was so irked by the incident that she was still hurrahing for Jeff Davis when she died in our Nebraska home in 1893. Out of love for Grandmother Elsie Shields, her grandson could have been no less than neutral, in his beginnings, toward the president whose agents had so angered his ancestors.

Now the name and fame of Lincoln were mounting to confute my youthful prejudice. One of my walks on the Fortieth Street Road I enriched by committing to memory the Gettysburg address. His inaugural "malice toward none" was to set a standard to which I could at least aspire. Lincoln was growing in the nation's mind and in the world's mind, too, as the ideal democratic man and citizen.

Here, silent companions on the open road, were three men standing uniquely together and alone, enlightening my world of

liberty. They were born within the span of eleven years—Lincoln,
1808; Thoreau, 1817; Whitman, 1819. They came into bloom
together in the darkening 1840s. Whitman and Thoreau were
friends. The prophet in Whitman saw Lincoln's greatness while
the rest were blind. He was to write at the martyr's death "When
Lilacs Last in the Dooryard Bloom'd,"—a deathless elegy in a
tragic hour.

These three poor and simple men, fruit of a single generation,
their greatness unseen in their lifetimes, emerge today as a towering trinity. They are America's gift to the world of a Moses, a
Homer, a Socrates. If my country notes and embraces them, it
will be health to its soul and marrow to its bones.

Thoreau was the only one of the three to be labeled by a
school. He made no capital of that. He wanted to live in his own
mind, not, as in books, in the minds of other men. To be himself
he sought the woods on the shore of Walden pond and built a
cabin home. He hoed his beans and watched with searching eye
the world of woods and wings. He lived free, asking nothing,
needing nothing, doing as he pleased.

He was crazy, the world he renounced was sure. Crazy as
Moses in the desert, Elijah in his cave, St. Francis in his her-
mitage. Find, if you can, a world-moving vision that had not its
source in solitude. He accepted, as the prophet always and everywhere has done, the penalty of his liberty. Refusing a demand
that affronted his freedom, he went willingly to jail. He wrote
books which no one in his day would read. He was living at the
roots of life and reporting what he found. By men living at the
surface he was laughed at. As I took to the road, he had been
"dead" a half century and his resurrection was at hand.

Walt Whitman, a Brooklyn carpenter, became a fitter of
visions as well as a joiner of boards. Deep down where men
really live we call the "grass-roots." Whitman, "away from books,
away from art," was down where the grass grows, down where
life flows, down where the people are. He became the prophet
of democracy, the spokesman for rough, free, common men and
for their comradeship.

He moved about the land, hailing its beauty, mingling with
its virile men. His mind was lighted, as he went, by a guiding

invisibility—a light, "rare, untellable, lighting the very light."
By this he was led, even as Thoreau, seeing "beyond the range
of sight," had been. How, but by an equal vision, can Lincoln
be explained?

My world had given me these three of the past for company
on the road. One living companion I must further note, a simple
senator.

Congressman-elect George Norris stopped in Lincoln in 1904
on his way to Washington, and reported himself to the press.
He was sitting, when I first saw him, in Editor Jones' office, a
plain man, not at all of statesmanlike pomposity.

I did not intend to like him. I took him for a routine railroad
politician, such as I was at war against. Norris could not be going
to Congress, I reckoned, save by consent of the Burlington. As
a judge he had been deliberate, I later learned, in issuing the
foreclosure decrees by which the burned-out farmers were being
separated from their farms. Nothing arbitrary, or lawless; just
deliberate. While the judge withheld his decrees, many managed
to raise the cash to renew or pay the mortgages and save the
farms. People have long memories for some things.

Having met George Norris, I proceeded to forget him. There
wasn't much a common congressman, fifty years ago, could do
in Washington. The House of Representatives in the first decade
of the new century consisted, roughly, of "Uncle Joe" Cannon
of Danville, Illinois. The speaker ran the show. The members
could run errands for their constituents and draw their pay.
Norris, of course, would humbly vote as "Uncle Joe" told him to.
With that I laid him aside.

Then came that day in 1910 when the sky fell. Of a sudden
Congressman George Norris pulled from his pocket a motion
that had the House and the country by the ears. He moved to
shear the Speaker of his kingly prerogatives. George Norris, without my dreaming it, had been in rebellion, all his years in Congress, against the old autocracy. He had waited his chance. Now
he had bearded the lion in his den.

I shared then, as I share still, the free man's dread of arbitrary
power. To preserve liberty, no person, interest or class must be
allowed the power to destroy liberty. Safety lies in keeping the

powers, whatever they may be, so balanced that none can tyrannize. Speaker Cannon and the elements behind him had more power than it was safe for any man or machine to have.

George Norris, to my delight, had turned out to be a henchman for no man or power. St. George of the dragon was to have in this George no mean follower. No one was more willing than I to magnify such a man into a Senator. The Nebraska majority for once agreed with me. Norris went on from there to thirty years of unprecedented service to the common man. He opposed, in 1917, our entry into the First World War. Nebraska joined the national chorus denouncing him. I did my own bit at that.

He came out from Washington, hired a hall in Lincoln, and hurled his defiance in our ears. The next year, the war over, we who had flayed him, for what I still think was his one great mistake, cheerfully reelected him. Here was a lesson I was to learn, a lesson for a politician and even for an editor. Men are not much given to punishing you for your opinions if they see you are fair, friendly, courageous and sincere in them.

A deadly rumor out of Washington was spread into Nebraska. Norris, the foe of crooks and purchased politicians, had sold out to eastern interests. The proof: a contribution, five hundred dollars, from a Pennsylvania businessman to Norris' campaign fund. The facts, happily, then appeared. That businessman had been ruined by the acts of a corrupt judge in Pennsylvania. He appealed for redress in vain to Congressmen from his own state. Then he appealed to the Nebraska senator. Norris found that the judge had had a money interest in the decision he had made. He saw to the impeachment and conviction of the judge and the restoration to the wronged man of his property. The contribution was a token of gratitude from the little man Norris had saved. The canard boomeranged.

Born poor on an Ohio farm, Norris was an incorrigible champion, as in this case, of the underdog. His instinct for discerning the public interest in any case was infallible. A freshman senator was advised by a veteran: "If you would be sure not to be betrayed by your inexperience into actions you will regret, watch Norris. Vote as he votes, and you will have nothing for which to apologize."

Through the years the senator spoke and wrote to me often of the pressures and temptations which warp men away from the high principles with which they come to Washington. The pressure of the party machine, the party contributor, the social bribe, the fear to fight alone broke the fine promise of many a well-intentioned man.

Almost single handed, Norris made the long fight that saved to the nation Muscle Shoals, root of the TVA. He stood alone, often, in Congress, but the people of the country stood with him. At the end, after his final defeat, I sat in his office and read till my eyes refused to focus the thousands of letters of love and gratitude which came to him from everywhere. He had been the senator for all the people of all the states. Why are there not more of them?

25

The wind blew a gale

THE PRAIRIE STRETCHED AWAY FAR, flat and dim in a January dawn as the train reached the little city of Bismarck, North Dakota's capital. The year was 1919. I had come to inspect a revolution which had the nation troubled and the prairie states agog.

The Bolsheviks had taken peasant Russia only two years before. While we looked aghast on peasant Russia going Communist, strange events were underway under our noses here. The farmers of North Dakota had of a sudden gone mad. Those hitherto unshakeable Republicans had swept the statehouse clean of Republicans. In North Dakota, of all places, a Bastille had fallen. What now? I was on my way to see.

Farmer Governor Frazier and a legislature of farmers led by Bill Lemke, a "renegade" lawyer, had gathered in Bismarck to tear down old North Dakota and erect a strange new state. It was not as if the people, in some fit of wrath had turned out recalcitrant Republicans merely to put in aspiring Democrats, the usual formula. The farmers of North Dakota were mad, but not as mad as that. They had been able to bring themselves to affront the faith of their fathers only by a more devious step. They had gone "non-partisan." Had they merely gone Democratic, horrid as that would have seemed to many good people, there would have been no call for the panic which the "nonpartisan" spectacle produced. The Democrats might have patched a few holes in the old garment of government. A new suit? They would never have thought of it. Now this strange Non-Partisan League thing, what mischief might it not do? I had hustled tremblingly to North Dakota, in the winter time, at that, to see.

This revolution, threatening the very fabric of our institutions, as apprehensive solid citizens everywhere were sure, had not, of course, been hatched full-fledged on the recent election day. To incubate an egg or a revolution takes time. It takes time—and suffering—most often in the form of economic suffering. Farmers, as everyone must know, are the most patient and long suffering of men. They may bark, but seldom do they bite. They vote, in all but times of unbearable stress, for the conservatives. We count on them to stand steady, stay hitched, even to stand without hitching, a barrier against change. In 1908, ten years before, North Dakota had voted two to one for William H. Taft for president.

By 1918 the patience even of the farmers had been strained to the breaking point. They held themselves exploited and abused by the interests in control of their economy. The railroads, the banks and the grain markets, they believed, had bled them white. What were they to do? To whet the farmer anger more, there had been their taste of war prosperity. As the First World War went on the farmers had known, for the first time in the lives of most of them, the intoxication of free-flowing cash. They had reveled for an hour in three dollar wheat. Suddenly the war ended. Down went wheat and the rest of the things the farmers had to sell. Down went the farmers. Their short-lived joy was turned to a weltering woe.

One always poor may be patient with poverty. To be contented poor, once having tasted riches, who is equal to that? To aggravate the farmers' woe, they were largely alone in it. While their income collapsed, their outgo for freight and interest and farm supplies remained even as before.

Arthur C. Townley had an idea. Let the farmers cease to imitate their sheep. They had voted as the politicians told them to, asking nothing, getting nothing for themselves. Let them combine and vote as farmers, even as other men vote as tariff seekers and wage earners. Let the farmers take over the state of North Dakota and make it work for them. Men in Model T's were set scouring the plains for members of the Non-Partisan League. Few farmers had fifteen dollars, the membership fee. No matter; a postdated check would do. They could have their political power on the installment plan as now we buy our cars. The plan went like wildfire or dollar-down TV sets. Here for the first time in our history, and thus far the last, was a political party financed by its own rank and file.

The plan worked. Amazingly it worked. Having invested their fifteen dollars in politics, the North Dakota farmers followed up their money at the polls. Voting for themselves, not for their old party, they swept the state. Now their legislature was meeting, raring to go. They would remould their world nearer to the farmer heart's desire. Was this bolshevism, transplanted to our own plains, threatening the foundations of our society? I was there to see.

The nation, it turned out, was in no danger. The farmers had nothing to hide. They invited me to their nightly caucuses briefed by Townley and Lemke on the next day's action on the firing line. It was no subtle conspiracy. A state of farmers was merely to be run by and for farmers, not by and for other interests by which they felt oppressed. It was a staggering problem. There were to be state grain elevators and state banks and state marketing in general and whatever else they wanted the state to do for them.

What came of it at last? Nothing much, as far as I was able, afterward, to learn. Nothing much is left of it but a lesson for all concerned. The political and business interests appalled by the farmer surge had learned it did not pay to let the farmers—or any proper interest—down. The farmers had learned to make their votes count; but also they had learned the limits, even as their adversaries had, of power. One extreme had led to another. The two clashed and crashed to the common loss, the way of all extremes.

26

A sound of revelry

THE WORLD TO WHICH I WAS BORN in 1875 was all but ended
a quarter century afterward. Darwin had won his way. The
scientist's solid pellet atom had softened to a whorl of electrical
energy. The automobile was a limping go. Big business was
looming, big government following.

Science had taken the stage held by theology before. It promised an earth so fat that heaven could be forgot. Progress was
the watchword, progress the chief end of man. Everything was
to be better. There would be better machines and more of them,
better houses, better health. Politics, along with the rest, should
be progressive. Above all was the higher and higher standard of
living to which we were to aspire. "Every day in every way," we
were chanting, "we are growing better and better."

The little mathematics I knew proved that, no matter how fast
and far we go, we can never reach the perfection of infinity. Jack
had tested that with his beanstalk, and the people on the plain of
Shinar with their tower of Babel. In the excitement of the change
in centuries, that did not trouble us. There was to be progress even
if perfection were impossible. With "Teddy" Roosevelt stealing
Bryan's thunder, setting a pace in politics, progress was the thing.

In the West we tagged ourselves Progressives with a capital
"P". Senator Moses of New Hampshire, a state politically im-
movable as its mountains, chose to call us rather "sons of the
wild jackass." That meant we were making progress. We were
getting under their skin. We followed "Teddy" with whooping
gladness. I voted for him in 1904 while my father looked on
sadly. A seed of his, voting for a Republican! My excuse that
"Teddy" was a very poor Republican, as most rich Republicans
then agreed, comforted him not at all.

With the Progressives splitting off from the Republicans in
1912, Woodrow Wilson, with his own idea of progress, his New

Freedom, rode in. The solidly progressive things he did! Not one of his New Freedom measures of forty years ago has been repealed or weakened. Progress, to this point, had restored a lost balance and prevailed.

Our dream of progress included a world free from war. The war on which we embarked in 1917 suspended other progress, but it was to lead to the foundation of all progress, peace. A war to end war, we called it. As the world was then, the dream could have come true. The dream was blighted. I, like many others, overestimated human capacity to sink ancient animosities in deference to new hopes. The war over, old politics resumed and we turned our backs on our plan for a lasting peace. In the mental and moral exhaustion which war creates, we elected a government pledged to go, not forward, but "back to normalcy."

Government and politics, under the progressive urge, had been improved and cleaned. A war had been fought without graft. Now through the gates opened by the rush "back to normalcy" poured hungry hordes long held back from the public trough. There was bribery in high places, theft of public property, crass spoilsmanship. The vultures were gathering. The Klan, sign of confusion and disillusion among the people, was riding again. States fell to its control. A terror, the rule of a hooded, darkness-covered mob, spread over the land. An attorney general went berserk, breathing threatenings and slaughter against all he chose to suspect of political heresy. To climax all this, the boom!

If we had forgotten our faith in an invisible heaven, our eyes were still fixed radiantly on an economic paradise. What Peter at his gate might yet dispense of eternal bliss on golden streets for saintly feet we did not greatly care. The gates of Wall Street opened wide to untold gold in hand. A president assured us that the business of America was business. When the soundness of the stock market path to bliss was challenged, the president stepped forth from his White House to reaffirm his faith.

Not all were present at this revelry. Our progress had brought effects which, in our celebrating, we had failed to weigh. With our machines we were putting forth more wealth than the people were allowed the means to buy. The people were going into debt

for their radios, cars and homes. The farmers, their incomes falling while stocks soared, were sinking in poverty. They asked for
relief. That was viewed as an impertinence. The farm relief bills
were vetoed by business-minded presidents. Government aid was
for seekers for tariffs, franchises, subsidies—not for the men of
the soil.

I wrote with tongue in cheek a screed which the *New Republic* printed, entitled "Stilts For All." Since the manufacturers
with their tariffs and others with their subsidies were raised by
government on economic stilts, I argued that farmers should have
stilts, too. How could the people keep their balance, half on stilts,
half on the ground?

Governor James M. Cox read the article and wrote me a letter.
That is how I came to make the one change of base in my
journalistic life; to work at the side of a man of such diversity
of genius and such driving force—statesman, journalist, businessman—as one may live a lifetime, travel far, and never meet.

The roar from the stock market rose till little else could be
heard. An election, in 1928, was to be held. What needed a candidate of the powers presiding over this heavenly dance to do
but point to stocks that must forever rise and never fall. Through
all the years from that November, 1928, I have heard in memory
a quiet, reassuring voice in its final radio appeal for votes, appris-
ing the people of the coming of the day, and soon, of an "end
to poverty." It was Herbert Hoover proclaiming the imminent
paradise. Eleven months later, 1929, the crash! Another world
had blown up under me. In hunger and despair we were learning once again: "Whatsoever a man soweth, that shall he also
reap."

So crashed the glittering world we had built on the shifting
backwash of a war. That war had paused, but had not been
allowed to end, ten years before. The good president elected in
1928 to celebrate the end of poverty found himself presiding,
in 1929, in helpless bewilderment, over an unprecedented, abys-
mal American misery.

For a measure of that collapse one must turn to ancient tales:
The tower of Babel which men in their pride had built, and the
confusion which came of it; that tragic Belshazzar feast with

men praising the "gods of gold, and of silver, of brass, of iron, of wood, and of stone," as we had boasted of our soaring stocks; then the handwriting on the wall, the crash! "What a fall was there," as Shakespeare wrote, when "great Cæsar fell!" Or John Milton's Satan conjuring his own proud heaven, even as we had been doing, and cast down: "From morn to noon he fell; from noon to dewy eve!" Yea, from '29 to '30, we fell; from '30 on to '31 we sank; then '32, then bottomless '33! So much for one house built upon the sand.

My horse and buggy world had yielded to progress—the automobile, airplane age. My world of progress, wheels against wheels, had led us straight to war. The war had indicted our progress. The more progress, the more war, and the deadlier. We would eat, drink and be merry, then, and die. On with the dance.

We had danced, the Armistice signed, "back to normalcy," to the year of my beginning, 1875. But that older normalcy did not trust in earth. This world was a wilderness of woe and not our home. We had set our sights on unseen streets above. That "normalcy" had been shot from under us in the war. It was the opiate of the people, men said, this putting off our triumph to another world. One world at a time, we said. We wanted our profit now. On with the dance! With a rush we got on. Some hurried irregularly and went to jail. So foolish, these, seeing how we could get ours merely by going in debt for stocks. So we blew our bubble. South Sea style it burst, and here in the pit we were.

As 1933 dawned on a despairing people my world confronted the motto of Dante above the gate to hell: "All hope abandon, ye who enter here." Of course, all hope was not abandoned. Before the collapse, one of our rosy philosophers, glorying in our bubble blowing, had warned us: "Don't sell America short." We had, in truth, sold America too "long," and for our venture were paying the penalty. What, looking deeper, we still could say was: "Don't sell the American people short."

More generously we could even say, "Don't sell any people short." The longer I live the greater has grown my wonder at the staunchness of human beings everywhere. The American people had only been waiting, as we weltered in the desolation we had brought upon ourselves, a clear voice to call us forth. A ruined temple was to be rebuilt. Without a leader would there ever be a mob to hurry us down to hell? Without a leader would there ever be a host to be hustled up to heaven? America heard the voice of leadership, rose to its feet.

The bubble of the '20s would never have been blown had we looked inside the book we praise the most and seem the least to read. In the earliest pages of that book we find the command which, with tragic results, we had forgot: "Thou shalt not muzzle the ox when he treadeth out the corn." It had been the fashion from earliest times to muzzle the men who tread out our corn for us. Whatever wage their hunger forced them to accept, we paid. Our era of progress had produced a change which made this old time muzzling of men a sheer insanity.

That change was quantity production, the revolution wrought by the machine. One good farmer with his machines could do the work of a dozen working with their hands. With labor in factories it was the same. Where goods had come in a trickle, now they came in floods. Muzzle the "ox," let him lack the means to own and consume these flooding goods, and your market is choked, your industry stalled. Crash you go in a 1929.

In our 1920's we had not thought of that. Who had? To hold that the consumer, not the producer, was the center of the economic round was as strange to us then as to hold, in the time of Copernicus, that the sun, not the earth, was the center of our world.

The fact as to the sun took centuries to be accepted. There are signs that we are learning faster in this matter of the ox and the corn. So now, yet another world awaits. With all our people, none muzzled, bargaining as equals, what excuse for another '29? Wisdom may yet work out a balance so stable, just and free we can take our living for granted and turn our freed attention at last to learning how to live.

27

The world of men

A FRIENDLY ARM HELD ME UP, that fire-lighted night of my first memory, to see the new puppy at the bottom of the barrel. With the touch of a human hand, whose hand I do not know, my remembered life began.

Another memory: A gentle face bent over me as I lay burning with fever in bed. That was John Wilson's stepmother come to ease me over what the wise wives of the Nine Mile community, the only doctors we knew, said was pneumonia. She made a tea of spruce leaves and charmed me into drinking it to make the perspiration come. She died when I was nine, and I grieved at her funeral as if I had been her son.

My Uncle Alex Reed could whip his weight in wildcats and, in his less sober moments, was apt to take on the task. But when he cut my hair he was gentle as a mother, though warning of the danger, if I fidgeted, that he might by accident snip off an ear. His wife, my Aunt Ellen, was a fair match, for fire, for him. She made for me, when I showed up at her cabin door, the best sorghum taffy that ever melted in a mouth.

I have told of the wall of cousins which, like the mountains around Jerusalem, sheltered me. There were the neighbors too, in the West Virginia hills, who flew to your aid regardless of blood. Yea, through all those hill-pent years I was a thread in a garment knit of flesh and blood. Then out to the stranger-peopled West! No one would know or care for me there. The prairie would bear me, the sky would cover me, the wind would lash me, but I would stand alone.

No! Jim Mussetter came at once to cart us off to church. Bill Bruce and Hank Smith appeared to teach me to row a borrowed boat. Friends soon surrounded us. The world, even the struggling world of the West, was not mere sod and sky and snow and strife. It was men and women as in the hills of home.

The new, hard world of drouth and dust was there, but a wall of men and women stood against it, broke its blows.

The men and women who formed the wall between us and the wind rise before me as I search my memory, a host of friendly faces with soft speech and kindly act. I shut my eyes and see them beckoning, I hear them singing—that song they used to sing on a Sunday baptizing day down on McKim: "Shall we gather at the river, the beautiful, beautiful river?" They are nearly all now on the farther shore. Are they calling me to roll up my trousers and wade across to them?

That was life in the country, a village life where men stood out like ants on a dinner plate. It would be different, I supposed, in the big world outside. There, surely, the institution, not the man, would count. The party would be bigger than the partisan, the church than the member, the corporation than the stockholder, the city than the citizen.

These people who had walled me in and held me up in the hills and in the village were common folk. They would lean on each other, help each other, as the way of strength in weakness is. In the big world of big men it would be each for himself. The wall of iron would end the wall of blood. But I was to learn what I should have known without waiting to be taught. Such a thing as the "common" people there is not, nor has ever been.

Charles Seckman, a tenant farmer, for whom, as a boy, I worked, was royalty. John Mussetter, quarryman, was a saint. Milo Sodgkins of the livery stable was a born leader of men, as was Frank Swarts, the section boss. There were all altitudes of us. There was no "common" man. I was to find uncommon men on the farm, in the church, in the factory, in the chamber of commerce—everywhere. Here was a sneak, there a saint, nowhere a "common" man. There was only at all levels the medley of high and low that makes up "man."

I was early concerned with parties, societies, institutions, states. Their progress, their fate lay heavy on my mind. I would study to improve that world. Now I look down the lane of retreating years and can hardly see that world for the people filling it. In age, even as in youth, I find a wall of flesh enclosing me, the world of men. A world healthy in kindness and diseased in hate!

World after changing world has enveloped me since my beginning in the hills. The hearts of men, "the universe grown conscious," through all the changes I have found the same. I scan the stories of the "realists," reeking with the stench of degraded women and scheming men. Some such I have known and suffered from. They have not been my world. But what a seething, diverse world this world of men has been!

In my Nebraska village Richard Andersen was a Dane and Grandpa Dougherty was Irish and Tommy Leray was French. There were Germans everywhere. The whole world was around us there. At the church we heard of Egypt and Babylon and Palestine. For Horatius at the Bridge and the fables of Aesop we had Rome and Greece to thank. A missionary, speaking in the church, made us aware of that funny people, the Chinese.

Yes, there were other countries and other continents. Yet the stars in the sky seemed hardly more beyond our world than these other countries and continents. The affair with Spain in 1898 forced the farther world upon us for an hour. That flurry was soon forgot. Then came 1914.

Joe Wurzberger, born in Germany, knew much that I needed to know and many a talk we had. He knew his Kant and quoted Schopenhauer by the page. He was a good American citizen. The Kaiser plunged into Belgium. I abhorred the act. Joe defended it. Our emotion was too deep for friendly argument. We continued to greet each other politely, but the old rapport was gone.

John Spirck was a friend from the time I was teaching little Saline County Bohemians. From him I heard with sympathy of Bohemia's long struggle for liberty. John Huss he made a hero to me even as to the Bohemians. I never tired of John Spirck's talk of his ancestral Bohemia. But John Spirck wanted America to go to war to free his Bohemia. I, like all middle westerners, far from the fire, was as passionately for peace. John Spirck and I still were friends, but our communion ceased.

Here was a new world of men to me. Through 1914 and on, my snug world, my insulated America, was passing out. The deep and lasting emotions, the fears and antipathies dividing Old World peoples, I could not, but for 1914, have dreamed. The opposing passions deep in my two friends had lain dormant, unseen by me, till stirred by the violence of war. The world abroad was not only nearer than I had dreamed, but in spirit more deeply cleft. Far away, in 1914, fled that brotherhood of man I had innocently thought was near.

When the war was won and a peace was to be made, more sober reminders came. We had counted ourselves, in America, evangels of peace. Now we were to prevent the peace. Old World emotions such as had divided my two friends from each other and from me cast confusion among us. The peace we were to make was only the provocation and prelude to another war.

To complete the disillusionment came our own peace-time witch hunt, the war's evil aftermath. War invokes the savage as well as the saint in men. Wars never end with the shooting. The Kaiser beaten, other enemies, even if we must invent them first, are to be fought and crushed. We had our citizens of German birth and ancestry. They had served their adopted country as well as we who were natives here. It was easy now for the tongue of terror, the mind of malice and of ignorance, to proclaim them false to us. A woman's voice reached me over the telephone. Was it true that Professor Virtue at the university was married to a German wife? The voice choked with horror at the thought of it.

That particular professor was a saintly scholar and his wife a saintly soul. What of that when postwar madness reigns? The wolf pack invaded the university. How frantically fearful of knowledge is ignorance! Blameless scholars everywhere were tortured by the persecutions of "super-patriots."

I was born into one after-war malignancy, that following the war between the states. In my middle years came this second postwar ferocity. A third such terror was to come on the heels of Hitler's war. My world, for all its saints, was still the wilderness of woe my Aunt Lide had sung about so many years ago.

28

The surging century

WE HAD LEAPED from ox-cart to rocket plane, from the speed of the tortoise to the speed of sound. The feeble muscle that wielded the ax in my boyhood hills grew into the machine with the strength of a thousand hands. Now we press a button and the might of the very atom itself obeys our will.

I need not repeat here how men have magnified their power. Our daily conversation tells of that. There has been more change (we call it progress) in my eighty years than in any ten centuries before. How came such magic in these years? The answer is so easy, so obvious, we marvel: Why wasn't it done before?

For all this new torrent of power has come from nothing but a simple turn about of mind. Men changed from egoistic guessing to patient, humble searching. Knowledge, we learned, begins with a confession of ignorance. Out of that the miracle.

In the world of eye and ear we got down from our proud toes and took to our humble knees. We said to this world our home: "We are not trying to command you; we are trying to understand you. When we have searched and found your ways, we shall find our reward in fitting our ways to yours." The men of the sailing ships of old must have had their inkling of this attitude. They could not command the wind. The wind bloweth where it listeth. But they could inquire of the wind and so set their rudders and their sails that the wind, whichever way it went, would bear them whither they might need to go.

Curiously, I was to find in old Scripture, guide to the world invisible, the clue to these new triumphs in the world visible. "Seek," we are told there, "and ye shall find. . . . Prove all things. . . . Hold fast that which is good." As the prophet had instructed the seeker of the soul, even so, to their glory and gain, the searchers of this world have done. Out of their seeking and finding, their proving all things, holding fast to the good, has

come the flood of knowledge and power which in my one lifetime has revolutionized the world.

By this way of seeking, putting unproved opinions behind us,
we have made ourselves partner with time and space. We have
multiplied our food and magnified our wealth. The very air we
have put beneath our wings. Maladies once fatal have yielded to
our questioning. At our humble knocking at the door, the holy
of holies of the world of sense, the utmost atom itself, has been
opened to us. This way of praying to our mother earth, not
ordering her, has yielded its wonders unceasingly. It releases a
flood of food. It speeds up the factories, producing, with less
labor, a mounting wealth.

Men through all the ages have been envious of the birds. They
flapped their arms and tried to fly and failed. At last, in my own
time, two men in a bicycle shop laid aside vain opinions and
sought the laws by which men might fly. Thus came, by this
simple way of humbly inquiring, a triumph the ages had been
waiting for. I have been allowed to live a neighbor and friend
of one of these two men, of that Orville Wright whose name will
be, like that of Icarus of old, a fable and a tradition as long as
the world shall stand. On a summer day in Geneva I was allowed
to meet that Albert Einstein, outstanding seeker of the age, out
of whom the conquest of the atom came.

Thus, in this world of matter, we have made the laboratory—
the testing ground, not the fighting ground—the way of
knowledge and the power knowledge gives. From this course,
result of a simple turn of our minds from our ego within to the
earth without, has come in these few years, triumph after triumph
in discerning the secrets of this world. The search has been
making us, as we seek and find its laws, one with our world,
partakers of its power.

Out of this search in the world of matter has come a peace.
Men disputed bitterly, before this way dawned, the shape of the
earth, the course of the sun, the substance of the stars. In my
childhood hills we disputed what creed of physician to employ.
Would an allopath or a homeopath best cope with our child's
diphtheria? Then came the way of searching, of ignoring guessings. The searching brought the discovery by which this terror

of childhood was dispelled. (An epidemic of it closed the school
I was teaching in 1892, leaving vacant seats when the school
could be resumed.)

For in this way of searching all minds become as one. The
world, with its one law, becomes as one. Men compete in the
search; they agree in the truth they find. We no longer hasten
stubbornly to believe. We wait to know. The world of science
knows no race, no nation, no creed.

Here now we stand, thanks to our seeking and finding and
proving, possessed of such power in the earth as could ease and
enrich us all. And behold, we stand aghast! We have hitched the
sun to our chariot, and we know not where to drive. Belatedly,
we see that, such is our ignorance and folly, this power may
serve, not to save and enrich, but to destroy our lives.

Caliban holds in his hands the thunderbolt of Jove. Must he
still be Caliban? Must the old divisions stand? I turn back to
the hills and seem to see there a hope. In my boyhood hills there
were, as I have said, the Baptists down on McKim Creek, and up
on Nine Mile Ridge the Methodists. I heard some little talk by
the immersers in the valley of the eternal peril of the baptizers-
by-sprinkling on the hill. The ridge had likewise its gentle doubts
of the more humid valley. But the argument, if any, was mild,
and more from old pride, I guessed, than present passion. No one
really thought that on these theological refinements our eternal
temperature was staked.

I observed that, whatever the neighbors may have argued in
theory, they held in practice to a common view. No one supposed
that my Uncle Tom, outstanding pillar of the church on the
drouthy hill, was destined to a less enthusiastic welcome at the
ultimate gate than my Uncle John, equally faithful to the deep
pools of McKim. Geographical expediency, not doctrinal compulsion, had in fact determined the difference between these two.
Uncle Tom lived on the hilltop far above, Uncle John in the
valley far below. Each followed his own level to his church.

I noticed that who moved from the hilltop to the valley was
soon found faithful and content in the new more aqueous brotherhood, and the other way around. When distance and doctrine
clashed, the doctrine stood aside. Then when ridge and valley

united at last to bid one of our number a sad graveside farewell, I heard no man ask how the departed had been baptized, but only how good a neighbor he or she had been.

Always, in my wilderness wandering, as I have often told, I have been asking the questions these pious people raised. Where did I come from? What is my business here? Where am I headed for? I did not see then, nor do I now, how one can evade these ponderings.

I asked these questions and had, from different directions, my different answers. I found conflicting opinions creating walls, dividing men. One answer to the riddle might serve the private comfort and character of those accepting it. But when, as so often it did, it shut away all those of different hope, it split the world into alien, hostile, unhappy elements. It laid the foundation for endless woes and wars.

The bloodiest of all wars, I was to learn, had been wars of extermination between rival faiths. A trace of such conflict remained between our two levels in the West Virginia hills, our two congregations of the West. The people, happily, were more kindly than their creeds. Commanders of hostile armies camped face to face have always had trouble to keep their men from fraternizing with the enemy. No difference of doctrine sufficed to divide us from the friendly neighbor next door. How easily men love each other, given half a chance!

There was Preacher Embree, rising above his preaching, refused to usher into permanent torment my friend Robert Haile, who had died under the delusion that he was an "atheist." And when John Gilgallon, a scoffer of scoffers, died alone and neglected in his shack, not a soul around but said there was good in the crotchety cuss, and hoped that God would be no more harsh with him than now his neighbors were.

There was the day I met on the street my good friend Father Bernard O'Reilly, then president of the University of Dayton and to be through later years an humble, faithful priest. Many a good talk we had had together and now I put a question which long had troubled me. "Bernie," I said (we were first-name-calling Rotarians), "you have been a good friend. You have been all kindness. We have never quarreled. You have shown in many ways that you wish me well. Yet, if I understand your soul's convictions, you are obliged to consign me, on the judgment day, to a most disagreeable eternal destiny. How can you do that to me, Bernie?"

Father O'Reilly looked me in the eye and grinned, a heavenly grin. Would any highest Judge, he said, condemn a man in my state of ignorance? "Neither do I condemn you," he said amiably; "go and sin no more."

Thus have I found men more merciful than their opinions, joining hearts across chasms contrived for dividing them. Moved by a vision deeper than their eyes behold, men join today in movements transcending old enmities.

In the year of my birth men were working to reunite what the strife of a decade before had torn apart. Steadily, since then, that Union has advanced in scope and strength. We have moved on to a friendly cooperation of our whole continent. We include in our circle of friendship our whole hemisphere. All this time, with ghastly groanings and disastrous setbacks, the whole world has struggled and stumbled in the direction of this same goal. Each of its wars, a bloody price for the self-made walls dividing us, has pressed us toward the unity we violate. With steady striving we beat at the barriers between us. At every fair chance we have pushed them happily aside.

This has been the central hope and current of my time. In an era of fast-emerging science, the free mind seems coming at last into its own. We have found the world of matter one body, subject to one law. The earth pays obseisance to one central sun. There is no one law for the valley and another for the ridge.

Searching out the laws of nature and conforming to them, we have vastly increased our power, our prosperity. But man, divided in spirit, though one in body, still defeats himself:

> *But man, proud man,*
> *Drest in a little brief authority,*
> *Most ignorant of what he's most assured,*
> *His glassy essence, like an angry ape,*
> *Plays such fantastic tricks before high heaven*
> *As make the angels weep.*

Yet have I not seen through all my years a movement like that with nature, though slower, toward a common center of the inner man? As if a compulsion contemptuous of the man-made walls dividing us were drawing us irresistibly together toward a central Sun!

29

Interlude: world of John Halcyon

IN MY WANDERINGS in the wilderness of this world, my home, I have been much advised, admonished and chided by a plain, quiet old fellow named John Halcyon. I have made some report of him elsewhere, and cannot omit him here.

One early summer evening, more years ago than I care to count, I was sitting on the shore of Lake Erie watching the terns at their fishing. I felt a tap on my shoulder. It was John Halcyon. He was glad, he said, to see me at last doing something well worth while. So saying, he strolled away, leaving me to the gathering dark, the whispering waves and the homeward-wending terns.

That was my first remembered meeting with John Halcyon. It was not by any means to be the last. He had a way from that time forth of turning up at the oddest times, in the queerest places, with the strangest things to say. He showed up one afternoon in Moscow, of all places in the world. I was walking from my hotel, the Metropole, toward the Kremlin, not far away, watching the careening motor cars and wondering that any pedestrian survived.

As I threaded the crowded street some man in the throng now and then would stop me, smile into my face and inquire engagingly: "Americansky?" As I met smile with smile I felt a tap on my shoulder. There was John Halcyon. I was seeing, he said, how the smile is a universal language. Were it allowed by master men, by governments, creeds and colors, to spread around the world, the world's troubles, most of them, would quickly be laughed away. With that, he vanished in the babbling throng.

I was at my typewriter in my newspaper office, pounding away angrily. Some one in the news reports had aroused my bitter ire. I was denouncing that some one in my best imitation of Horace Greeley or Henry Watterson. I would scald that bird in print till every feather of him would fall away. A tap on my shoulder, and there stood John Halcyon. "Why so hot, little man?" he said, and vanished through the door.

There was an early morning in Switzerland, the east a growing glow. As I came forth for the freshness of it, there stood John Halcyon, pointing. Far away, where he pointed, snow-capped Mount Blanc was towering, a shining city of sun-lit golden streets. A moment before a wall of clouds, as usual, had curtained it. For one glad instant I gazed, then the mists swept in and all was grey again.

"Now you know it's there," John Halcyon said, "though you never see it again."

His friendly tap on my shoulder fell as I watched the moon rise over the ocean in Florida. He caught me up sharp that day in Washington I fell into a political argument. Did I not know, he warned, that I only expose the ugliness of ego when I argue? No one talks sense in argument, least in political argument.

There was that special time when John Halcyon looked over my shoulder and found me reading *The Open Road*. If only, he said, we would take to the open road, the open mind, the open heart, we should become such men as this world has never known, men time could never obliterate. Glad to live, not afraid to die, on the open road we should be healthy, free, happy, invincible. Yes, even immortal, John Halcyon said. That was the America to work for, he went on, a land whose business is building men—men for this world, men for that. He turned and left abruptly, as if abashed by his own eloquence.

One hot July day I came upon him in a field, listening to an insect uproar as if it were a Beethoven symphony. I had been thinking of how, of a sudden, in my last summer in the hills, the sassafras thickets and the weed-grown old fields resounded with that same sizzling. It was the year for the seventeen-year locusts, as we called the cicadas then, to come forth and have their day and say. They clung noisily to the blackberry vines and preempted every bush. They drowned out the bird songs and all the sweeter summer sounds. Then, as suddenly as they had come, they were gone.

We plucked from the weeds and bushes the empty, transparent garments they had left behind. The expanding life within had burst the imprisoning shell and passed on to other forms. Through the years of their exile these creatures had lived in the dark earth. Did they argue as to that, their home? Then, argument or no argument, an urge implanted in each one there in the dark led it to move up till at last it burst into the light of another world. Now here they were, basking in the sun of heaven, drinking the ambrosia of the sassafras, singing their delight in the new home they had found. John Halcyon was listening, smiling, rapturous. "A parable," he cried. "So men, too, rise from old worlds into new, from darkness into light!"

Often, when I walked in the woods, I would find John Halcyon there, sitting on a log, listening to the cardinals, watching the chipmunks, soaking up the sun. It was good to be there, he said. The world was too much with us. The very next day, as I hurried down Main Street, who but John Halcyon should hail me reproachfully. "What's the rush?" he said. "You'll be the same fellow, only older and wearier, when you get where you're going, as you are here."

An unashamed backseat driver he was, speaking out to remind me of the world I was missing as I raced, unseeing, along. He himself was never hurried, worried or angry. Nor was he troubled by such doubts as nagged at me as I journeyed in my wilderness.

And so, the day the word came that my Aunt Lide had died—died happy, the message said—I was glad to feel the familiar touch on my arm. I would put the issue squarely up to him. He was so sure of things, let him clear up the mystery, the question of the worlds, so puzzling me. What was it made clear to him what was all cloud to me? John Halcyon laughed a little and then, I thought, something glistened in his eye. There is no secret, no mystery, he said. There is only the stubbornness which keeps us from opening our eyes to see. "O Jerusalem, Jerusalem!" he cried.

He waited a moment, then went on. In his youth he had heard great talk of this world as a wilderness of woe, of this world not our home. They spoke of a bright world unseen, like that early morning mountain vision he and I had had in Switzerland. They talked of that world and what it required of us here, and as they talked they fell to arguing and even to fighting, for as to the laws and geography of the other land and the road thither they violently disagreed. And the more they talked and quarreled about what was right and true, the less they seemed to practice what they preached.

Perplexed at the dispute, John Halcyon had said to himself: Why not find out for himself what that world was like and which way lay the road thereto? What need to ask if fire is warm and ice is cold? Let him find out for himself. Just so he did. He tried loving his neighbor as himself. It worked. He liked the way it worked. He felt better for it. It must be right.

He tried putting himself last, the great Idea first. Again he felt repaid. Something within him said it must be right. How could himself be miserable, John Halcyon said, when he isn't thinking of himself at all? One article of faith after another John Halcyon tried, holding fast to what proved good.

So that was the secret of John Halcyon. What the rest of us talked, he tried. Thus the two worlds came to meet and agree in him. This world he wore lightly on his outside as he wore his coat. As to the other, I heard him saying something from his beloved poet about his "interior soul impregnable," and how "nothing exterior shall ever take command" of him. He was the friendliest, freest man I ever knew. He did what his manhood bade him do, no more, no less.

As age bore down on me, John Halcyon seemed to renew his youth. He showed more and more of that young spirit to which, the Scriptures tell us, wisdom is most easily revealed. I can only describe him as one who, losing himself, had found himself. How he got his earthly living I never asked or knew. That seemed to be the least of his concerns. The way of the lilies of the field appealed more to his interest. As far as I know, that rich, yet happy man had nowhere to lay his head.

30

Singers on my way

CARL SANDBURG came to our town a-singing. That's the way, as of course we know, all poets came at first. A born poet, even if he could not read, much less write, could sing. He came along singing and so we had Homer and the Iliad and the Mikado's wandering minstrel and the rest.

So Carl Sandburg, who can read and write (how he can write!), came to our town with his harp, singing the lines the rest of us could only read. It was my happy lot to introduce him to his expectant audience. All I can remember of my introduction is its two short opening sentences. I said: "Beware the poet. He is dynamite."

The rest can have been only an elaboration of that theme. Most of us skate on the surface. The poet dives and soars into the heart and height of things. What he sees today the rest of us, if we do well, will be seeing in one hundred or maybe ten thousand years. The poet, in short, is forever pouring the new wine of the future into the old wineskins of the past, and great are the explosions that makes. Thus the dynamite. I may have found the words for it first in the lines of an English poet of a century ago. Arthur William Edgar O'Shaughnessy has the poets saying:

> We are the music makers,
> And we are the dreamers of dreams,
> Wandering by lone sea breakers
> And sitting by desolate streams;
> World losers and world forsakers,
> On whom the pale moon gleams;
> Yet we are the movers and shakers
> Of the world forever, it seems.

Carl Sandburg, "common as old chips," as my mother would have said, as simply Lincoln-like as the Lincoln he brought to

life in epic books, came shuffling on the stage with his guitar.
Of what he said and what he sang I haven't the least memory
now. What matter, that? What a man is, is thunder over the
whisper of what he says. There Carl Sandburg stood and talked
and sang, and the world of sham, of hypocrite powers and white
sepulchres, was moved and shaken as he stood. The man himself
was a song, even without words.

This great factory we call the world is stingier in its output
of poets than even of diamonds, of Joans d'Arc and of the Socrates. I count myself fortunate to have met four whom I knew
as poets. (How many more poets born to sing unseen I may have
met can never, of course, be known. There were millions of
them, I hope.)

There came a wisp of a woman, singing, to our town. Edna
St. Vincent Millay, too, I was privileged to introduce to her
audience. My life since that event has been a sad regret that I
had not the sense to repeat one little rhyme of hers and then sit,
harmless, down. That tiny gem would have been this:

> *The world stands out on either side*
> *No wider than the heart is wide;*
> *Above the world is stretched the sky,—*
> *No higher than the soul is high.*
> *The heart can push the sea and land*
> *Farther away on either hand;*
> *The soul can split the sky in two,*
> *And let the face of God shine through.*

Had I done that, and it resulted in one person in that audience
troubling to memorize and ruminate these lines, it could have
been one soul saved.

What she said and sang there, as in the case of Carl Sandburg,
I forget. She was nervous and shy. A pig may be phlegmatic and
serve its purpose well. Not so the poet poised to transmit to our
dull ears the music of the spheres. She worried for her audience.
Were they too hot, too cold? So worrying, she worried us. There
is no report of poets as particularly happy folk. Caught as they
are between earth and heaven, with the tongues of immortal
angels and the tempers of mortal men, a certain tension in them

can be understood. Pegasus, the winged horse, had to his harm
to come down to earth to feed. Here was a nightingale caged in
a frail human form. She sang and we all sang with her, however
silently. That incubus of a body she was soon to cast away. The
voice is singing to us still.

Hervey Allen of *Anthony Adverse* fame lived in winters in
a grove of Florida pines. He himself wrote some poetry, just
enough to make him a friend of Robert Frost. Hervey wanted
the poet for a neighbor and so Robert Frost had a cottage of his
own in nearby pines. There on sunny winter days Hervey Allen
could submit his prose to Robert Frost and Robert Frost could
show his newest poem to Hervey Allen. There was a neighbor-
hod rumor, once, that the friendship was clouded for awhile after
a tired Robert Frost had fallen asleep one evening while listening
to Hervey read his latest manuscript. A bit of neighborly malice,
I must take that rumor to have been.

A frequenter of that vicinity, I had some talk with the terse
poet of California birth and New England life and mind. He
was the man who held "good fences make good neighbors," the
poet who, in a crowded age, wanted only to be left alone, a
Vermont marble of a poet who so soars without quitting the
ground that the honorary degrees of the colleges cover him as
leaves the autumn earth.

George William Russell, born in Ireland in 1867, came to
our town lecturing in 1928. That was my one sight and sound
of "AE," a poet future ages will prize beyond the vision of our
own. He was sitting on a sofa in the lobby of the lecture hall with
a fountain pen in his hand, such a long pen as was never made
in America. Around him we flocked carrying books of his poems
to be autographed. He was good naturedly swinging the long
pen in the effort to oblige us all. Often since I have seen crowds
in like manner surrounding a hero in search of autographs. The
besieged is most often a prodigy of Hollywood or the athletic
field. Not once since that night in 1928 have I seen, or even heard
of, a poet so pressed for his favor.

The mathematician, with his effort to reduce all life and
nature to a single equation is, we are told, the epic poet for the
atom age. No more Homers; no more Miltons with their thun-

dering words. The man with his plus and minus, planning the electronic intellect, is to do our singing now. But in 1928 at least one poet could draw an admiring crowd, prizing his name on the fly leaf of a book.

The obsolescence of the species might have been seen then in the poet's beard, making a necktie a superfluity. There was about him an all around atmosphere of days long gone. His lenses were small and metal rimmed. His coat, though of good quality, had a look of day before yesterday. His trousers bagged at the knees. All this you could see and contemplate only before meeting him. The Rubicon of introduction passed, externals were forgot. This shaggy man, all soul, was all that counted then.

It was not George William Russell in name we met. That name had dropped from him when first the Irish youth began to write. To the world of readers he was only "AE." It was "AE" I was called upon to introduce. To him, as to Homer and Carl Sandburg, poetry was music. He chanted his lines in a high but mellow voice which lulled as music while it stirred as thought. Here was a minstrel to whom here and there, and now and then, were all as one. As to earth and heaven we heard him asking:

> *Or am I there already, and is it Paradise*
> *To look on mortal things with an immortal's eyes?*

So went his songs and my ear was not quick enough to take it in as fast as he gave it out. I arranged to meet him next morning for a leisurely interview. I remembered a poem of his, an eight-line picture of a man—any man—who is blind to a world he will not deign see. He gropes his way through dark and cold when all around is unseen light and all within an unfelt warmth. The tragedy of it:

> *He turns away, through the dark to roam,*
> *Nor heeds the fire in his hearth and home.*

I asked "AE," once we were settled in his room, about this little rhyme and its origin. He reached for my volume of his poems (I was an autograph hunter, this time, too) and in the space below the poem on page 152 he wrote in a sharply angled, sloping hand: "He came to his own and his own received him

not. The light shines in the darkness and the darkness compre-
hendeth it not." The poem was the New Testament book of John,
compressed into eight short lines.

"AE" retained my book and went on to talk. He told of his
years scouring Ireland on a bicycle organizing the farmers into
cooperative societies, the better to cope with their poverty. We
think of a poet as living with head in the clouds and feet dangling
off the ground. Here was a poet whose feet were firm in the
soil of Ireland. If his head, nevertheless, reached the clouds, that
was by grace of the tallness, the greatness, the limitless reach of
him. He did not believe, he said, that men could thrive and
survive for long with their feet on pavements, off the ground.

As he talked, "AE" drew from his pocket a box of vari-
colored crayons. Opening my book he began a scratching there.
In a trice the title page was dark red cloud in a dimly blue sky,
a rolling mountain range behind, a foreground of weeds and
stones, and in between a space of what might be red-blue-green
water. He signed the picture, "AE."

"See," he said, holding it up to me, "a bog in Donegal."

For "AE" was a painter as well as a poet. There were long
periods, he said, when nothing worth putting into words would
come to him. At such times he would paint. The bog in Donegal
he could see and paint at will. That world lay outside of him.
He could go to it. The vision from which the poem comes
emerges from within. You cannot hurry it. You must wait for it.

He turned the leaves of my book, searching for picture space.
He set his crayons going and soon I had a plowed field with a
rustic gate with boulders for its posts. And then again a bleak
Irish seacoast, boulder strewn, made while he remarked that no
one had ever found a fourth generation Londoner. That city soil
could not reproduce itself.

He returned my now priceless book, this man with feet in
the earth and head in heaven, and we went our separate ways.
He was to leave this life soon afterward. He would not be much
concerned at that. He was not one of the stumbling blind men
he wrote about so pityingly. To him, here or hereafter made little
difference. "The fire in his hearth and home" was, here or there,
the same.

31

Makers of a world

A CIRCULAR SWING, progenitor of the merry-go-round, was the central attraction of my first "Fourth." "Twenty-five times around the world for a nickel, half a dime, the twentieth part of a dollar," went the barker's cry.

A horse pulling a sweep about the centerpole supplied the power. A wooden cogwheel at the base of the revolving pole recorded the revolutions, the one mechanical computer of my day. There were to be twenty-five times around, no more, no less, for the precious nickel paid.

A platform for the square dances, which were all the people knew, supplied activity for the irreverent. The church folk frowned on dancing, an invention of the devil, and mourned for the souls of such as engaged in it. Here was the first lemonade I had ever seen. Seeing was all. It cost five precious cents a glass.

For the rest, we gorged on the chicken dinners we had brought and rejoiced in the visiting with distant neighbors hardly to be seen save as the Fourth came round. There were no traffic casualties worse than aching corns, for all came horseback or afoot. There was singing and speaking of pieces. One celebration, I remember, was opened with a prayer.

The Fourth, when I reached Nebraska, was in great vogue there. The numerous veterans of the late war made this a day of patriotic zeal. Towns planned community celebrations for purposes both patriotic and pecuniary. The noise our ardor yielded was rising toward the roar which led to the agitation for a quieter, "sane Fourth."

Every smallest community had, in those days, its blacksmith or two. Wherever there was a blacksmith and his anvil, an impromptu cannon was at hand. The blacksmith's anvil had on its face a square hole to receive the handle of its metal-cutting part. Fill that hole with gunpowder, set another anvil over it,

lay a train of powder away from the charge. Heat the end of
an iron rod red. Touch the hot iron to the powder train. The
ensuing explosion, sending the upper anvil high in the air, was
a delight to the small boy and an inspiration to all true patriots.

The Fourth of July firecracker, straight from China, had now
appeared. A packet of fifty was only five cents. As economical
a boy as I was obliged to be could have a fairly furious day on
two such packs.

The serious meaning of the day was still, in the Eighties,
emphasized. No Fourth was quite itself without a recital of the
Declaration which gave the day its start. The fashion had waned
before I was old enough to claim oratorical honors for myself,
but I listened with open mouth and ears to the young man in
a Prince Albert coat whose celluloid cuffs rattled their own
applause as with waving arms he defied King George III and
all other enemies of liberty. As, with the years, the patriotic
prayers and perorations faded, the noise of the celebrations grew.

The turn of the century found Aguinaldo in rebellion, in
the Philippines, against our venture in colonialism there. What
should the wretched rebels do but quote against us our own
words, the foundation of our Fourth. Our Declaration had said
that governments derive their just powers from the consent of
the governed. Now look at us, governing the Filipinos against
their will! What was a bearer of what we called "the white man's
burden" to do but frown on the circulation there of the Declaration as a seditious document? The less we sang, on our Fourths,
about the rights of men, the greater the noise, on the Fourths,
we made.

The dynamite firecracker arrived with its special din—and
death. The harried citizen spent the great day with cap pistols
at his head. Street car rails were strewn with noise exploded by
the wheels. A Fourth of July was a siege of Sebastopol.

On the day before each Fourth, through those years, I was
printing impassioned editorials begging the children, old and
young, not to blow themselves up on our happy Independence
Day. The day after the Fourth I was pointing with horror to the
previous day's fireworks casualties, even as now our traffic tolls.
The Fourth had become a day of terror. In honor of the freedom

the Fathers had won for us we were shedding about as much blood as the men who died to make us free.

Thus far, our country has survived its recurring excesses and inanities. It took twenty years and many laws and much arguing, but at last the Independence Day bedlam quieted down. The appeal for bloodless highways takes the place of prayers for a sane Fourth. Gone with the passenger pigeon is the Fourth with which my life began. The parade, the spread-eagle speech are past. The firecracker is frowned upon. The day remains a valued reprieve from labor. We prize it especially when it falls on Monday, bestowing the long weekend for which our taut nerves yearn. Are we forgetting the meaning of the day?

In 1900, when still we celebrated with dynamite and eloquence, there were one hundred and fifteen lynchings here. The next year there were more. Forty-five years later the lynchings were down to twenty. Another decade and there was only one. Now there are years with none.

The Philippines are free. The women vote. Slowly our social castes dissolve. We have fought and won two wars against aggressive tyranny and have survived more years of totalitarian cold war. Our Fourths resound less of liberty, yet liberty, always in peril, plods painfully on.

What was it kept us, spite of all our digressions, so firmly on the path? What but the men I have witnessed making up my world!

I loved the woods and hollows of the hills and yearned for them long when they were lost to me. I loved the white light on the green prairies of the empty West and the stars so close above them in the night. The fields along the Fortieth Street Road remain a grateful memory.

Yet all these wane, in the perspective of the years, into a mere background for the world of men. Close up, never fading or diminishing, stand the men and women who walked with me the long way I have come.

The old schoolhouse sheltered me without, but Harve Hamilton and all the teachers fortified me within. I have a friendly memory of the Nine Mile church where John Poynter, the preacher, sought to scare me into heaven. Far brighter the memory of my Uncle Tom who kept the church warm and the lamps alight.

The way has been lined with institutions, parties, societies, machines. They had their use as tools—tools never better than the lives employing them. I remember the carpenter, not his saw. Men, not machines, wonderful as these tools have been, have made my world. I give thanks to the men who have made and kept my world a scene of hope, freedom, opportunity.

I was born in a darkening time. The moral lapse which follows war had reached, in 1875, its depth. Walt Whitman, with his bold call to a free manhood, a healthy democracy, had been dismissed from his government clerkship as a dirty-minded man. Lincoln had been killed. Men whose malice he had restrained were glad. It was the day, in business, of the Jay Gould, the Jim Fiske. Politics had sunk to a sordid traffic in offices and privilege. A noted senator was to call purity in politics "an iridescent dream."

Slowly we were to rise from that morass. Grover Cleveland broke forth with the radical doctrine: "A public office is a public trust." Carl Schurz and the mugwumps pressed for civil service reform. Henry George was warning that back of all worldly problems lies the question of the land, man's common inheritance. That issue has been from his day to now overturning old world governments. Our day to face it cannot always be deferred.

Susan B. Anthony, showered with chivalrous scorn, was starting the shrilling that was to win for women their political equality.

Such men and women stand forth as forward leaders of my age! Among these was my neighbor Bryan, no massive mind, but a mighty figure with his tongue. Privilege, dominating politics, was ruling with too high a hand. Bryan sparked the opposing fire. Theodore Roosevelt and Robert La Follette followed to feed the flame. When Woodrow Wilson came to reflect into law the minds these men had made, our democracy reached a new level not, to this day, lost.

A bright womanly figure shines from a dark Chicago slum. Jane Addams, with the heart of mercy, was salvaging the human wreckage of a harshly rushing age. On Morningside Heights a great mind wrestled with the rising problem of the age of machines. How fortify men to face the new world fronting us? John Dewey, for the teachers, was answering. Out of Cambridge came William James, his *Varieties of Religious Experience* bearing broad knowledge and tolerance and friendly understanding, without loss of faith, in a sadly bitter field. I think of Booker T. Washington, a gulf-closing patriot; of John P. Altgeld pardoning the Chicago "anarchists," giving his political life that justice might be clean; of James M. Cox, walking open-eyed into defeat for the sake of a league of peace; of Franklin Roosevelt, with glad abandon putting men above mammon (how for that he was hated, loved!). I put these down with Einstein the immortal (to its glory our country gave him refuge); with the silent scientists who have magnified our knowledge, strengthened our arms and undermined our ills. Last and not least, the millions who, "nameless, unnumbered, the long hard pathway trod," the followers who made the leaders possible.

All these and unnamed many more have served to raise in these eighty years the level of our life. To them my gratitude.

32

The outside of the platter

THE HOOPSKIRT, when I first looked around my world, was in its expiring agonies. Already it had shrunk far from the haystack dimensions of the decade before. The modest bonnet, tied by ribbons beneath the chin, was giving way meanwhile to a thing of bolder brim.

The workaday sun-bonnet, curving over the head and face and floating down the back, was much longer to endure as a defender against freckles. The shoes the women wore were high-topped, as became a country infested with copperheads, but not high-heeled. Their Sunday skirts, in that modest age, allowed but the tips of toes to show, then trailed off far behind. The dragging trains swept the footpaths clean, uniting style and service in a potent partnership.

The silk hat, the stove-pipe as we called it, was a staple covering for men of dignity up to the day of Chester A. Arthur as president. For the minister it was a must. No man could be a pillar of society without his topper to prove his rank. No disguise served better the sharper, the scalawag, the charlatan than a piously respectable "high" hat. With the "topper" went perforce the black Prince Albert coat. In a pinch the cutaway would do. Without a cutaway, with pockets in the tail for handkerchief and lunch, I could never, at sixteen, have maintained the decorum and discipline of the school I was called to teach. The high silk hat had so declined that I was to miss that dignity. The derby had come, instead, that dome of iron to hedge our bulging heads.

I had a narrow escape, meanwhile, from the obsolescent Prince Albert. My tiny school of orderly Saline County Czechs gave way to the much larger, more explosive school at the village of Princeton, nearer home. Here were seventy-five pupils of all ages and grades to sit upon. I figured that nothing but a black Prince Albert could preserve me here.

My good friend Harry Farquhar, clothing salesman par excellence (He was earning a hundred and fifty dollars a month when I, a teacher, felt rich at fifty), talked me out of it. The time had gone, he said, to pass in that disguise. Irreverence was scoffing at that pretence. He sold me another cutaway.

With the split tail coat went, of course, the derby hat, congress shoes (Elastic tops allowed you to pull them on and off without benefit of buttons or of strings) and a boiled stiff-bosomed shirt. A stand-up collar and string tie topped it off.

The women, all this time, had been evolving, too. The hoopskirt shrank, but it was long before it let appear that the women's feet were corporeally linked with their upper altitudes. The wasp waist, meanwhile, was the thing. Here, while science was proving that all the world was one, the women set out to make every one of them two. With gasping zeal they sought to bisect themselves. They tugged with red faces and bulging eyes at constricting corset strings. Nothing more spacious than a segment of spine should bridge their upper and their nether parts.

The balloon, banished from the skirt, sped upward to the sleeve. Votes for women would no more have worked in the balloon sleeve day of President McKinley than in the balloon skirt day of President Abraham. No woman so expanded could in either case have inserted herself into a voting booth.

From "stove-pipe" to no hat at all; from high top boots to sandals; from swallowtail to shorts; from boiler plate to sport shirt—so men's changing envelope. The women? From hoopskirt to hobble; from wasp to nature's waist; from high-piled hair to close-cropped head—anything, everything, given years enough.

As soon as I felt equal to it, at about nineteen, I embarked on a moustache. All the boys courted moustaches. The more daring ventured chin whiskeys, too. But whiskers for men, all but unanimous in hoopskirt days, were going out, along with the women's bustles, as the motor car came in. The doctors with their dignity were last to let whiskers go. Benjamin Harrison, elected against my solemn protest when I was thirteen years old, was the last of the bewhiskered presidents. The moustache, mine with the rest, followed, into desuetude, though less universally,

the hair-entangled chin. Only a thin scattering of men, most of
them scientists fleeing from the witch hunters, hide behind
whiskers now.

There were ominous portents, in the mid-nineties, of shocking things to come. The bloomer girl well nigh blew down the
town. She was promptly, the huzzy, stepped upon. The newspaper which I was later to serve narrowly escaped a libel suit
when it named a teacher as having come before her classes in
a divided skirt. All this time the women, if they powdered or
painted their faces, did it mildly, surreptitiously. I remember
with horrow the first time I saw a woman brazenly reddening
her lips in the public gaze. She stood in a doorway in Hot Springs,
Arkansas. A perfectly respectable doorway, too.

I was still capable, as I learned then, of shuddering. But that
was long, long ago—more than thirty years. I was still capable
of consternation when, a little later, in a lawful St. Louis restau-
rant, I saw a young woman caressing a cigarette. In my childhood hills my sainted Aunt Charlotte had modestly "rubbed"
snuff. Many older women there solaced their lingering years with
a tobacco pipe—clay or corncob as the case might be. I really
should not have minded the lady in St. Louis with the cigarette.
But here was a miserable guilt-by-association circumstance. This
was far from being my first sight of a woman with a cigarette.
The spectacle in St. Louis carried me back to the old, half forgotten days when I was a newspaper boy. As I trod with my
papers my morning *Journal* route (so early in the morning) my
path was often crossed by certain furtive women turning night
to day. They were invariably smoking cigarettes!

Inside the kaleidoscopic coverings, the transitory bonnets of
these years of my life, and along with the new ways, were there
corresponding interior changes as the world reeled by? Do the
clothes make the man as some have said? They have made, if
they do, strange men and stranger women in my day. Myself,
I have not found them strangers. The surface changes. The heart,
as if eternal, stays about the same.

33

The crash of worlds

A KING WAS A RULER who had a right to cut off your head whenever that suited him. I had read in the Book of Proverbs: "The
wrath of a king is as messengers of death." It was terrifying. The
world, in that day, was full of kings.

Germany had its kaiser, Russia its czar, Turkey its sultan.
China, Japan and Austro-Hungary were headed by emperors.
Italy, Great Britain, Spain, Brazil and Portugal had kings. Lesser
potentates loomed everywhere. In those days we sang in church:

> Each breeze that sweeps the ocean,
> Brings tidings from afar,
> Of nations in commotion,
> Prepared for Zion's war.

That was a pious hope. The nations were to come running
to hear and heed what our missionaries preached. Little could
one not a prophet have dreamed of the commotion which really
lay ahead. Napoleon III of France had headed, five years before
I was born, the procession of discarded kings. A pause, then,
while the storm was gathering. I was old enough to read the
news for myself when Emperor Dom Pedro II of Brazil was
sent back, in 1888, to Portugal, and the republic was proclaimed.
That ended monarchy in the Western Hemisphere.

The industrial revolution running high in the western world
was to have its impact on the thrones of kings, on the power and
perquisites of feudal lords, on the control and conduct of governments. No power in government, however complete, can go
on unchanged when the lives and conditions of its subjects greatly
change.

Storms were rising then in the absolute Russia of the czars
and in the relatively free, yet still measurably feudal, British
monarchy. Turkey under its sultan was "the sick man of Europe."

The democratic stirring inspired by Giuseppe Mazzini was still moving Italy. The conglomerate state of Austro-Hungary was seething in every part. Ralph Waldo Emerson had remarked in his Boston Hymn, on New Year's Day, 1863:

> *God said, I am tired of kings,*
> *I suffer them no more.*

Time proved our philosopher had read the divine mind aright. Down, seven years later, went Napoleon III. Down, in 1888, went Pedro II. In 1911 down went the Manchu dynasty in China. Soon came, concomitant of the new economy, the First World War, and the falling stars became a shower.

No throne in all the world stood firmer, as the year 1914 began, than that of the emperor of Germany. Now power overreached itself. In 1918 that throne crumbled and the kaiser was in Holland, a fugitive. Down with Wilhelm went the Hapsburgs. The Czar of Russia had preceded them a year. Four years later the sultan was out and Turkey a republic with the rest.

From those days to now the crashing of kings has been constant. Such as survive remain, as in Britain and Scandinavia, as amiable figureheads. They reign. The people or other powers rule. No most timid lad needs fear for his head in the presence of such royalty as now remains.

Each breeze that swept the ocean has brought its tidings of nations in commotion. Kings, when the peoples were stodgy peasants, bound to the soil, would do. When men began to stir about in motor cars and fly on wings of their own making, kings, throned and unthroned, crowned and uncrowned, fell. The upward thrust of the under folk toppled ancient thrones.

In all this, America led the way. The vanguard republic, an adventure shocking to old world kings and lords, set a pace the whole race was to imitate. Our Constitution set going a tidal wave which has circled the entire world. We called that beginning the Revolution. It was a revolution which was seldom to pause and never to cease. Throughout my years it was moving at rising speed. At no time has it been safe to settle down and say: "Soul, take thine ease." Say that, go to sleep, wake up, and the world has passed you by!

For a rigid mind, unable to adjust itself to the swiftly changing life around, these have been hard, unhappy times. They have
seen a steady broadening in America of the base power. There
was from the first a rising power of the people, marked by such
names as Jackson, Jefferson, Lincoln. That rise has been speeded
in my day. We have been riding out a storm, an expanding
democracy.

Some of the peoples have overthrown their kings only to fall
victim to yet more ruthless powers. This we have thus far escaped.
We could yet fall victim to some disease of democracy—the
deceits of the demagogue, the temptations and compulsions of
the plutocrat, our own indolence. The rabbit in the field and
freedom in the world live alike dangerously.

A glorious adventure! It would not be an adventure if it could
not fail.

In our winter debating societies in my Nebraska village we
faced the possibility that it might fail. The signs of the times,
did they indicate the downfall of this Republic? Furiously we
battled, pro and con, two champions for the affirmative, two for
the negative. It was no idle question then. So near the Republic
had come to falling but twenty years before! Among our debaters
were men who had retreated at Bull Run, who had tasted the
woe of the Wilderness, the heartbreak of Fredericksburg. We
had seen the Republic totter. From a harder blow, surely, it
could fall.

Whatever the perils then appalling us, there are others the
future could bring. In the years since those debates I have seen
the Republic, in the eyes of the apprehensive, die a thousand
deaths. Every election year, to hear the partisans, the fall of the
Republic is imminent. Still the Republic stands. Shouldn't we
cease our debating, our worrying?

Who knows but it is our debating, our worrying, that keeps
the Republic still upon its feet? How do we defend the life of
anything—a crop, flower, tree, child, home—but by watching
close for the dangers, the diseases, by which it might be harmed?

I note one book, more praised, I fear, than obeyed, which is
replete with warning how peoples in the past have failed. There
was that Sodom which, for its people's perversions, was consumed

by a sudden fire. The fire which singes any other Sodom may
not be sudden. It is no less sure. There is the roster of kings in
this book who did right (or evil) "in the sight of the Lord," and
who triumphed or fell accordingly. If they were to thrive they
must "do justly, and love mercy, and walk humbly," regarding
their neighbor as themselves. This done, they stood. Failing in
this, they fell.

I note among us now a certain preocuupation with food and
drink and the cravings of the flesh, with a heaping up of wealth
and power; and a certain story in the Book frowns out at me.
That wild party of a proud, rich King, the thousand lords and
their bedizened ladies praising the gods of gold and silver, of
brass, of iron, of wood and of stone.

Then the handwriting on the wall: "Thou art weighed in
the balance and found wanting. . . . God hath numbered thy
kingdom and finished it."

It can happen. Even as my village folk of seventy years ago,
we might well scan signs.

34

The good I've seen

MY FAVORITE COUSIN IN THE HILLS, young Emma Reed, stood too near the open hearth and her cotton dress took fire. She ran to the creek in front of her house and leaped in to quench the flames. It was too late. She died in agony. My Uncle Will came walking feebly up the hollow where we lived, coughing as he came. He had come to visit my mother, his sister, then go back to his Marietta home and die. He was one of the myriad victims of what we called consumption. My cousin, Earl, likewise coughed his life away. Our drinking water on the ridge came from springs; in the valley, from the creek. My father was one of many to take to his bed with what we called the fever—typhoid, of course.

A log he was sawing on a hillside broke loose and rolled over my cousin, Frank, dealing a permanent injury. A dead branch of a tree fell on our neighbor, Mrs. Fleming, as she did the family washing in the shade. When I revisit the old cemeteries of my boyhood memory I note the number of headstones with lambs chiseled on them. Such the mark of the old time infant mortality. Death dogged our steps and sorrow, whether in the hills or on the plains, was never far away. What of good can I remember out of all this?

I remember with a touch of joy as wholly good our chief common interest and activity there. That was our neighborly service to the afflicted, the sorrowing. All of us were poor, yet none went hungry. In helping one another, in that world of heart to heart, we found deep comfort. The "wilderness of woe" was lightened and brightened by the sun of sympathy.

The woe was not good. My world was to labor mightily to ward those woes away. To our attacks on poverty, our defeats of disease I need not here return. Our neighbor needs us less. We may be a good neighbor, not by nights sleepless with the sick, but by writing in comfort at home a check for the Community Chest. Our next door neighbor may need us less, but who is our neighbor? The calls for our help and sympathy grow wide as the world is wide. With all our gains, my neighbor is unhappy still. His way through the wilderness still is dark. I need not wish to have my neighbor weep that I may have the pleasure of wiping his tears away. There is weeping a-plenty still. The peoples enslaved by their masters; the spreading of tyranny everywhere; the Germans falling into Hitler's trap; master men and demagogues forever luring and driving men; our unceasing groping in the dark for the clear path through the wilderness! All the room in the world remains for that human help and sympathy which stands an undoubted good.

What then of the farther good toward which my world has worked? Our wealth has multiplied. That has not been enough. Those who gain it live in dread of losing it. Those who lack it live in dread of not gaining it. We have gloried in our speed, only to bleed on the highways. We strive for what we call security, only to find the clouds of world-ending wars looming over us. These goals for which we have fought have been found wanting when won. What has been left to be accounted good?

So much there has been to test! It has been a dizzy age. I have been Eliza—*Uncle Tom's Cabin* Eliza crossing the river down at Ripley on the floating ice. With each step more slippery than the last, how sure was the shore? World after world has swept by me. To what end? To what good? The time to take inventory comes.

I begin with that neighborly service and sympathy in the hills. That was a gold no age can corrupt. The same good heart of us has shown itself since in our times of catastrophe—our winds, fires, floods. It even showed in those tragic emergencies, our wars. War abroad, so bitter as a whole, has had its precipitate of sweet, the harmony it yields at home.

Every friend I have ever had goes into my inventory as a lasting good. Would I had deserved more of them! They include, of course, my father, mother, aunts, uncles, cousins. Most of those friends, as must be with old folks' friends, are beyond the curtain now. Each one as he goes leaves this side the veil the poorer, that side the less a doom. These live still in the memory they enrich. I walk with them, talk with them, still. This communion, I trow, could turn out to be of more substance than we may count on now.

Every bird whose flight I learned to know remains to me a good. The early trillium, the fire pink, the bloodroot, the violet were good beyond dispute. When my child was born I said surely here was good supreme, he and she who brought me him. Even so, with the years it proved. Here was good compounded. It was to bring the gentle mate of the boy and the grandchildren, delight of age. Finally, most priceless, the liberty to which I was born and which it has been my happiness to preserve.

At this accounting of the good which I have found and proved I could go on till time to blow the candle out. The books grown better, the faith grown brighter with the years! The songs, the symphonies which sweeten the memory! The green of the grass, the sunset's red, the full round yellow moon! Each year's new martyrs, known and unknown, yielding up the grosser for the greater good! Behind all dross, such gold!

My world grows more and more bewilderingly complex. The essence of good is clear and simple still. "What doth the Lord require of thee?" So simple and great the good I have possessed —and plentiful, and cheap! "Tis only heaven that is given away." "How cheap is health, how cheap nobility!" Such billionaires, if only we had known it, we have been.

A gladsome, sobering fact: This wealth of good is as near (but no nearer) at the end of the rich, tumultuous progress of my years, as it was for my Aunt Lide, or any of us, in the poverty of plains and hills.

35

The world to come

THERE I STOOD, a tow-headed boy, watching my Aunt Lide chop the wood for her supper fire, singing in her sad, sweet voice:

This world's a wilderness of woe;
This world is not my home.

Here now I stand, at the summit of my years, surveying the world I have wandered through, pondering the world to come.

My Aunt Lide was soon to lay her armor by, as she longingly had sung, to "rest in peace at home"—whatever that unseen home of her hope might turn out to be. I was to plod on, trying out the world at hand, shaping it as best I could into a home. Aunt Lide and her generation had despaired of this world. They had turned for their hope to another world to come. My times were to turn to what we accounted a more substantial hope. We would build for our enjoyment here and now the home of the heart's desire. One world at a time, we said. That other world, if such there were, could wait.

We had a mighty new strength for building this new world. The explosive power of the free, inquiring, tolerant mind, the "scientific mind," was now at our command. After ages of blind groping and ignorant guessing at the nature of the world around us, this new approach to knowledge was coming, at my beginning, into full acceptance and full play. The old, vain disputings of fixed opinions as to nature's laws had given way to humble questioning. We were becoming not merely loud proclaimers of opinion, but quiet pursuers of the truth.

The results as, of course, we know and boast, were magical. So exploring our world, finding its laws and conforming to them, we were able to make nature's powers our own. Strength of muscle, our reliance in the hills, was magnified by the power of the coal, oil, steam, electricity. In the end we pierced the very holy of holies of the world of matter, the atom at its heart. Boundless power, at last, was ours.

Chop wood for the supper fire? The Aunt Lides of today press a button and the supper fire is lit. The food my Aunt Lide earned by sweating summers with the garden hoe, her great granddaughters pour effortlessly from a can. I have told how a steam-driven machine reprieved me when a boy from sweaty labor with blistered, bleeding hands on a quarry concrete pile.

We went on to foil the fevers, massacre the germs. We drained the swamps. We watered the deserts. We harnessed the rivers and put the sun to work. We lengthened life that the Aunt Lides might longer grace this world turned heaven in our hands. We heaped up gold and multiplied our speed. Faster and faster we went, racing with the sun. We learned to get our bread with no least sweat of brow. A little more heart in spreading the goods our power creates and we shall have ended poverty. My poor Aunt Lide, fussing about another world when this one, as we have transformed it, could have been hers.

Such were the miracles we wrought. Alas! How little I need now to describe our disillusionment.

Boastfully we had built a tower to reach to heaven. Our tower scraped the skies and lo, here was not paradise, but the same old distracted, battling Babel of a world. We had often enough been told: Man cannot live by bread alone. Bread had been so precious, so hard to get, we would not believe it. Now the well fed world is here and our hearts are still hungry. For all our drinking, we are still athirst. In our gilded houses we are not yet at home. Something is wanting in the world we have so marvelously built. We are empty pitchers. We are a fireplace without a fire. We have learned to make a living. We have not learned how to live. We can fly. How fast and far we can fly. But whither should we fly, and why? As our new joy is, so our new sorrow is. As our power is magnified, so has our peril been.

The key to the ultimate riddle, "the chief end of man," we had neglected, with all our searching, to seek and find. For want of that wisdom, our new-found powers threaten to be a fatal enemy instead of a saving friend. We find ourselves children with bombs sputtering in our foolish hands.

Worst of all, our souls, not less than our bodies, are found in jeopardy. In piling up our power we are delivering ourselves over to great machines—machines of metal and machines of men. In the days of our weakness we were poor, but we were free. No man, in my cabined boyhood hills, was in the power of any other man. Now, gripped by these machines, one man must submit to some other man and all together must bow down to the machine. We are servants of the powers we have erected above ourselves. Thus our secret souls are menaced, even as our bodies are, for only in liberty can the spirit live.

So stands our world today; and what is this we hear? In all their myriad tongues the peoples crying, as my Aunt Lide was singing in her world of long ago: "This world's a wilderness of woe; this world is not my home." What now? Where do we go from here? What of the world to come?

Down on McKim Creek at Baptist baptizing time we sang of old a song with the challenging refrain: "There's one more river to cross." Today as we survey this triumphant yet defeated world of ours there is clearly, ere we reach our promised land, yet another river to cross. I venture here my guess as to what that waiting Jordan is.

By the magic of our new-found free and searching minds we have possessed ourselves of magic power in the earth. As all human experience has proved, power without the wisdom to wield it is a peril in itself. It is that peril hangs over us today. It did not occur to us, in the ardor of our pursuit of power, to employ the same magic key to open up the vision safely to govern the power of our hands. The means of life we know. The ends we still murderously dispute. So now we find ourselves a bird with but one wing. Before we can safely fly we must add the wing of wisdom, the wing of the spirit, to balance the body we have so greatly magnified.

What does this require of us? Merely by the skilled, tolerant, searching which has wrought such wonders in the visible world to explore with equal diligence the unseen world out of which spring wisdom and will. Such searching has brought unity and peace in science. Why not in the region of our conflict, our suicidal strife?

The search itself can bring the peace we must have to make this world a home. Men searching humbly for the truth do not battle bloodily over rival guessings at the truth. The search itself will preserve that liberty which the corporate life, the age of the machine, tends to destroy. The very spirit of the search entails a free mind, heart, and tongue, which no power can ever bind. Such moving in step as may still be required of us can be the willing marching of free, upstanding men.

What gain, beside that innate in the mere seeking, may we expect from this searching of the life beyond the eye? Our seeking into this world, as we have seen, has won its way to nature's ultimate secret, the heart of the atom itself. May a corresponding goal await this other search? That is for the searchers, each for himself, to find. To feed their hope this can be said: Through the ages intrepid men of divers lands, languages, and times, many of them held in worshipful memory today, have ventured far on this way. With one accord they have reported back the assurance: "Seek and ye shall find."

In a world torn by proud, angry opinion, resistant to reason, is all this asking the impossible? It has proved possible in one world, the world of power; why less in the other, the world of the spirit? What else is left to do? What is this but our "one more river to cross"? Here rests the hope for the home we seek in our world here. Surely we may seek it, assured that the truth found here will still be true in whatever world is waiting farther on.

My world and my Aunt Lide's, so tried and found wanting, was the century of the body. What hope now but to make the world to come the century of the soul!